ADVANCE PRAISE

"Urgently needed, deeply human and transformational."
CORREY VOO, Investor and entrepreneur

"Beyond Words *is the missing piece of the puzzle. In our distracted and hurried world, the importance of relationship is powerfully and practically brought to life."*
PATRICK MAWHOOD, VP Product, RX Global

"An inspirational, practical pathway to a better way of working and living. Simultaneously disruptive and healing, the book challenges outdated narratives, offering a new vision and template for human relationships."
PHIL HAYES, Author and founder of Management Futures

"Kerry-Lyn has written the gold standard in Beyond Words *that teaches you how to become a great leader based on her science-backed Relational Wealth Strategy."*
CHRISTOPHER KAI, Speaker and #1 international bestselling author

"Beyond Words *is a paradigm shift; a brave new way of supporting the corporate world in the midst of a digital revolution. This book offers a practical way of showing how the quality of the way we relate can become the competitive edge, not just today but in the future."*
LAUREN, SVP top 10 global investment bank

"What I experienced reading Beyond Words *was formative. It developed my understanding of people and enlightened me about my own career – why the bad was bad and the good was good. What I have been able to do in the short few weeks of reading this book is nothing short of amazing."*
ALAN CREAN, CRO, BridgingX

Published by
LID Publishing
An imprint of LID Business Media Ltd.
LABS House, 15-19 Bloomsbury Way,
London, WC1A 2TH, UK

info@lidpublishing.com
www.lidpublishing.com

A member of:

businesspublishersroundtable.com

ISBN: 978-1-918215-13-7
ISBN: 978-1-918215-14-4 (ebook)

BEYOND WORDS

How to Lead People from **Survival** to **Success**

KERRY-LYN STANTON-DOWNES

MADRID | MEXICO CITY | LONDON
BUENOS AIRES | BOGOTA | SHANGHAI

CONTENTS

ACKNOWLEDGEMENTS

I have always known this book was never really going to be written alone. Yes, my hands typed the words, and I spent countless hours creating the language and crafting the framework. The truth is every page is the result of the countless nervous systems that have met mine, shaped mine, steadied mine and held mine when I could not hold myself.

This book exists because of the people who crossed my path long before I understood the language of regulation and connection, or the power of the relational space. Those early experiences – some painful, some profound – became the first teachers of my nervous system. They showed me what it was to shut down, to run, to fight and, ultimately, to discover the unexpected relief and regulation that occurs when people offer presence, curiosity and belief instead of judgement, defence or withdrawal. Because of these experiences, I learnt to regulate what once overwhelmed me, to trust what once frightened me, and to believe in what once felt unobtainable.

To those people I owe so much – and there are a few I want to name. To my husband, **Stephen Stanton-Downes**, my greatest champion and challenger, whose unwavering belief in what I wanted to bring to the world helped carry this work long before the world realised it needed it. To **James Scroggs**, the great disrupter, who reminded me that disruption, when done with heart, is a gift. To my dear friend and colleague **Rickie Simpson** – for your sharp mind and humour.

To **Ros Draper**, for the hours of conversation that shaped my thinking. And to some of the greats who lit the path

– **Martin Buber**, **Harville Hendrix**, **Dan Siegel**, **Stephen Porges**, **Bruce Ecker** and **Hedy Schleifer** – your wisdom fuelled my curiosity, expanded my lens, and offered space for questions that informed how I wrote this book.

To **Adam Strange** and **Sophie Bradshaw** of KA Writing – thank you for helping me structure and language the stories and principles in a relatable, grounded way. To **Hannah Hargrave** and **Phil Hayes**, who each held the faith long before a publishing deal existed. To **Martin Liu** and the team at **LID Publishing** – thank you for providing the mechanism through which this message can be shared with the world; your commitment and care helped make the intangible real.

And to every client who has sat opposite me over the years – your courage shaped these principles.

To you, the reader holding this book right now – I hope these pages do more than simply inform you. I hope something touches you – softly, truthfully, humanly. Inviting you into a deeper conversation with yourself, with others and the extraordinary space that exists between us.

FOREWORD

BY STEPHEN STANTON-DOWNES (FOUNDER AND CEO OF BRIDGINGX)

Over the last 30 years working in tech, consulting and entrepreneurship, I've seen teams tear each other apart. I've seen leadership groups unable to execute the things everyone knows they need to do. Not because they lacked a desirable proposition. Not because the funding wasn't there. Not because the business strategy was poor.

These were teams filled with bright, capable people, often with top-tier educations and pedigree logos on their resumes.

So what's going wrong?

Quite simply, they could not navigate their interpersonal differences – and turn those differences into strengths. When pressure rises, people slide into fear-driven survival states. Individually and collectively. And once you're in that state, the organisation is starved of the abundance-minded energy needed to adapt, create and succeed.

In larger organisations this becomes a slow poison. They can limp along for years, even decades, buoyed by brand momentum, market position or competitive moats. Consuming more energy than they produce. Becoming unpleasant places to work in ways that only reveal themselves once you've lived inside them long enough.

In start-ups, this dynamic can be fatal. There is no surplus energy. Every conversation matters.

So what is this troublesome thing we need to name?

We've traditionally called it 'culture' – a catch-all bucket for everything that isn't process, people or systems. But that's far too vague to be useful, and with the science now available to us, it's no longer good enough.

What Kerry-Lyn does in this book is narrow the field to something precise: the quality of the way we relate. How we show up with each other. How we regulate and co-regulate. How our nervous systems collide or collaborate. And then she gives us a set of personal and team practices that dramatically increase our ability to regulate, relate and perform.

I know with certainty my own business may not have survived without this approach. And I believe those who have worked with me would wholeheartedly agree.

So what can you expect?

Firstly, do not underestimate the apparent simplicity of the 8 principles of Relational Capacity. They are powerful and will act as your handrails through the liminal space you are about to enter. They've been stress-tested from every conceivable angle by thousands of conversations and interactions and can be applied everywhere.

What this book will offer is a systematic way for you and those you lead to face your challenges differently – with clarity, courage and connection rather than fear and reactivity.

This work is timely and desperately needed. Leaders today face a heady mix of complexity, pace and change – mental health, inclusion, inter-generational differences, geopolitical volatility, and the unimaginable acceleration of technology and AI.

Perhaps the expression, often attributed to Peter Drucker, that 'culture eats strategy for breakfast' needs an update. Culture emerges from how we relate. Strategy only succeeds if we relate well enough to execute it.

To have any chance of succeeding, we must become deliberate and methodical about how we relate. And for that, we need a framework – a language for naming the unnamed. For going beyond words.

What the framework in these pages provides is a path between traditional HR or change-management thinking and the worlds of coaching or therapy. It is implementable at scale, while still deeply human. It is grounded in the biology and neurology of the relational brain.

This work enables us to address what leaders have long known undermines performance and success – but have never had a practical way to act upon.

And, spoiler alert, you may find it changes the way you lead your life too.

INTRODUCTION

RELATIONAL POVERTY

When I first started bringing my work in relational psychotherapy to organisations, I noticed the workplaces I visited had something in common. In every boardroom, at every meeting table, and in every office, a quiet epidemic was raging. And while each office had its own specific symptoms – a burnt-out workforce here, dysfunctional team dynamics there – the overall illness was the same. Everywhere I looked I could see the impoverishment of our mental health.

Poor mental health is bad for business. It not only makes people miserable at work, more likely to call in sick and more likely to leave, it also impairs productivity, decreases efficiency, and reduces profit. And yet what I was seeing first-hand is what pervades almost every organisation in every industry in every country today. In some it shows up loudly – in the form of stress, burn-out, anxiety, and depression – and in others quietly – in the form of difficult relationships, unhealthy competition, disengaged employees, and disconnected teams. The result is not only unhappy staff at a lower level, but whole organisations operating at a fraction of their true capacity.

Of course, this isn't news. In the UK alone, mental health absences, high staff turnover, and spiralling health insurance costs lose businesses more than £50 billion a year. Despite witnessing it first-hand, I don't believe mental health is the problem at all.

It's merely a symptom of something worse.

Our society has led us to believe we are the 'main character'. We've become used to prioritising our own needs, seeing the world through a lens of our own boundaries and demands. We're taught to manifest our success, protect our time, create tribes around us of people just like us. We use social groups to enhance ourselves and build ourselves up, withdrawing with ease from those who have a 'problematic' point of view.

Even our language of self-care has been weaponised. We label others as 'toxic' or 'narcissistic', while absolving ourselves of accountability for the way we show up. If I don't like something, it's a 'you' problem, and at the same time I can continue to 'do me'. In all of this, we polarise the 'other' and seek our own safety, power, and protection.

And yet we've never been more self-interested, disconnected, individualistic, and afraid.

As easy as it is to believe this is the scourge of our current age – a problem caused by social media and technology – this obsession with self is more innate than we think. In the 1950s, sociologist Erving Goffman wrote about our human fascination with how we are perceived by others, and how we actively work to shape these perceptions in our conversations and interactions. In this way, we are intrinsically 'self' conscious – viewing the world only from the perspective of 'How am I doing?' rather than asking: 'What could be happening here between you and me?'

I believe it is this individualism that pervades our teams and organisations like a cancer. Poor mental health, burnout, anxiety, disconnection, and disengagement are not the problem, but the output. In other words, the real root cause of our mental health disaster is not the inner workings of isolated brains, but the fact that those brains have become isolated in the first place. By removing ourselves from relationships with others – through increasing polarisation, digital separation, constant mitigation of risk, the hurtling speed of change – we've removed ourselves from the one thing we need to survive: connection.

This may seem counter-intuitive. Aren't we, in this day and age, more 'relational' than ever? We live in a hyperconnected world. We're no longer bound by geography; we can work in multiple teams across disparate locations; we don't even have to leave our desks to reach out to our colleagues. In many organisations, we've replaced problematic hierarchy with 'agile teams', protocol with values, prejudice and exclusion with diversity networks and support systems.

Aren't we more connected than ever?

Much has been written about communication at work. There are scores of books on how to build 'empathic' organisations, to create cultures of belonging and psychological safety. Yet what if all our efforts to 'fix' ourselves and our workplaces are based on a fundamentally outdated and flawed understanding of what the brain really is?

What if we don't know who we are at all?

As you read this book, I want you to be prepared to change everything you think you know about the way we work in teams and organisations – because, rather than being based on an individual shift, this is based on the fact that, as psychotherapist Thomas Fuchs said, 'the brain is a relational organ'. This means our wellbeing is 'embedded in the meaningful interactions of a living being with its environment' – in other words, our brains enable our interactive processes and are, in turn, formed and restructured by them. No matter what we do to try and 'fix' ourselves and the way we work, no matter the amount of 'rewiring' we do, nothing will change unless we learn to be with others in a way that fills us up rather than depletes us.

I believe the mental health epidemic we see in organisations is an output of what I call relational poverty. As humans, we come into existence, not inside our mothers' wombs, but in the social and emotional spaces where we meet each other. For this reason, we need a new way to talk about our relationships at work, a fresh paradigm where our ability to relate to our colleagues is more important than our fixation on ourselves.

This means setting down the individual model and accepting the truth that we are who we are because of the way we relate to others. You cannot talk about anything in the world of work without talking about relationships. We can address individual behaviours, values, and culture all we like, but we will never solve any of our most pressing problems – performance, hierarchy, job satisfaction, efficiency, growth, competitive advantage, innovation, performance, risk management, talent retention, engagement, digital transformation, technology adoption, automation, scalability, diversity – not one single element of operating in any organisation in any industry in any country in any economic or commercial conditions – without understanding the way we interact.

BEYOND WORDS

Although we will talk a lot about language, this isn't a book about communication at work. Language is and remains a key part of how we relate to each other, and choosing our words often allows us to choose the impact we have on the people with whom we interact. It also allows us to label, to express, to categorise, and to have a fundamental impact on our responses and the responses of others.

But language also reduces complexity, forcing us to translate our physiological, individual experiences into mere words. As a result, we're often at a loss and ask ourselves,

How can I communicate my deeply felt experience in a way that's understood? And how am I supposed to do that at work?

This book goes beyond words. It takes us to an understanding of the *process* of how we relate to those around us. Yes, words might give us a vehicle of expression, but until we can use them in service of hearing, understanding, and finding out about others, they won't give us the connection we need. As humans, connection is our innate desire. As well as making us happy, it makes us more productive, more efficient, more creative, and more collaborative. Our brains are wired to be in relationship because it's only in relationship we become the best version of ourselves.

In Japanese culture, there is a concept called *Ma*. It refers to the space between things – the meaningful emptiness that creates harmony. *Ma* might be the emptiness between structures in architectural design, the pauses in music or theatre that allow the performance to shine, the negative space in the art of flower arrangement, or the art of restraint in a ceremony or performance.

This book is about how we show up in that space. My hope is that, as you read these pages, you will take away more than a collection of tips. I hope you will find a deep-felt sense of being able to improve the way you show up in the relational space so that you are not just a participant in conversations, but an effector of change.

Our experiences of a conversation, a meeting, a review are often not in the words, but in the process of connection or disconnection in the space between. That's why this book goes beyond the words and instead focuses on the felt experience of what happens when we show up or not. I believe this is the key to transforming not only individual conversations but meetings, relationships, teams, and whole organisations, because the most successful teams don't just 'communicate well' – they create a space where others feel seen, heard, and psychologically safe enough to contribute at their highest level. When leaders understand this, entire organisations can change.

I appreciate change is hard. The eight principles you will learn in this book are direct and practical – even at times uncomfortable. They require grit, resilience, honesty, and commitment: as my colleague Jean Gifford says, 'brain power and heart depth'. They are also highly effective. When you learn to apply them – and, more than that, to *embody* them as a different experience and response – you will see they are transformative both on an individual level and at the level of your whole organisation. This is because, as well as having the ability to rewire our brains, we have the ability to rewire the space between us, too.

As you read, I want to challenge you to an experiment. At the end of each chapter from 4 to 11 is a section called 'Start with This'. As you come to each of these sections, I challenge you to try the exercises I have picked out, to do just one thing that will start to improve the way you relate to the people around you.

See what happens.

As you do, I think you will start to see why the traditional self-help model – 'fixing' the individual with a view to making us happier, more palatable, less problematic – is not only the wrong answer, but also the wrong question. The real solution to the biggest threats to our workplaces is not rewiring the way we think.

It's stepping into the space between.

CHAPTER 1

RELATIONAL BEINGS

*"In every encounter there is you,
me, and the space between."*

WHAT ARE WE GOING TO DO ABOUT JILL?

Over Christmas and New Year 2023, I remember having a series of conversations with my husband about a problem he was having at work with one of the directors of his company. On walks with our extended family and during evenings by the fire, we would often find ourselves returning to the same conversation, which generally began with him saying: 'What are we going to do about Jill?' In the end, it became a sort of running joke. Whether he was about to talk about it or not, every time my husband sighed, we would all pre-empt him and exclaim 'What are we going to do about Jill?'

But underneath the laughs, 'What are we going to do about Jill?' was a serious question. Jill was a fantastic director on many levels. She was innovative, precise, ambitious, and analytical. But she had, in my husband's words, some 'learned communication tendencies'. She would talk over people in meetings, give unhelpful feedback, and railroad colleagues into agreeing with her. Not only was Jill's communication style getting everyone's backs up, but it was also holding her back in her career.

Jill had already been given very clear feedback. She'd been told that her dogmatic approach wasn't working for her colleagues and direct reports, that it was making them feel irritated and defensive. She'd politely been asked to hold back a little in meetings and let others give their points of view. But it hadn't worked. As my husband told me, 'She just doesn't seem able to change. It's like she's not *listening*.'

At around the same time, in cities across the UK and the US, 12,000 Google employees were receiving a company memo. As their eyes scanned the email, they saw phrases like 'We hired for a different economic reality than the one we face today' and 'We take full responsibility for the decisions that led us here'. Then came the paragraph they'd been dreading: 'We'll need to make tough choices...'

Sure enough, the memo culminated in the announcement that those who were receiving it were having their roles 'eliminated'. The email signed off:

> *To the Googlers who are leaving us: Thank you for working so hard to help people and businesses everywhere. Your contributions have been invaluable and we are grateful for them.*

Just like that, a decade or more of work was reduced to an impersonal email saying they were no longer needed – but thanks anyway. Google, the company that promised to be a family, to create the perfect work environment, to 'respect each other', was dropping its employees without so much as a phone call.[1]

In the weeks that followed, former employees took to social media to share their experiences. One software engineer recounted on LinkedIn, 'So after over 16.5 years at Google, I appear to have been let go via an automated account deactivation at 3 a.m. this morning.' He was, it turned out, '100% disposable'.[2]

It wouldn't be a stretch of the imagination to suppose that the following few months were hard for those former employees. Their confidence was low, their mental health in tatters. But the reality is that, for most of us, it doesn't take a redundancy to make us feel that way about work. A recent survey of employees across the UK showed that poor mental health was the number-one reason for employee absence, costing employers £51 billion a year. A full 29% of Generation Z say they feel ill-equipped to deal with workplace stress.[3]

For managers, dealing with employees' mental health is one of their biggest challenges, and companies are scrambling to promise mental health support as part of their onboarding packages – even before an employee has started at the company. How to balance the needs of employees with productivity and profit has become the main dilemma facing leaders in organisations across the world. And it's not going away.

For Jill and her colleagues, for Google and its employees, and for workers at all levels across the globe, something has gone horribly wrong.

FROM MENTAL HEALTH TO RELATIONAL POVERTY

One or more of the three scenarios I've described above might seem depressingly familiar: personality clashes threatening effective leadership, the objectification of employees to the point where they feel disposable, the poor mental health of a large proportion of the workplace. They're hardly surprising, and they're hardly rare. But when you look at them closely you can start to see that these three examples might not be separate issues at all. In fact, they might easily be one issue which is simply manifesting itself in a variety of ways.

Let's look at them again.

When Jill spoke over people, railroaded them, or simply ignored their opinions, her colleagues felt unimportant and diminished. Not only this, but they began to believe that Jill thought her opinions mattered more than theirs. They created a narrative around Jill's behaviour and character that led them first to disengage from her and then to question their own competency and value. They felt frustrated that they couldn't share their contributions, which caused them to disengage from their colleagues, their companies, and their roles within them. Individualism stifled innovation; politics overtook productivity. Talented members of staff were even threatening to leave.

If we look carefully, we can see a similar situation at Google. When they received a simple memo telling them of their redundancies, employees who had given many years' service to the company felt unimportant. Disposable. Their sense of worth was destroyed, not just because of the redundancy itself, but because of the relationally poor way it was communicated. This feeling of lack of worth caused by the absence of empathy in that communication followed those employees out of the door. It made its way onto social media, to dinner parties, and into conversations with other members of the industry. For the executives writing that communication, their focus had been purely on getting the job done in the most efficient way. They didn't know these people personally. They were just on the other end of a Zoom call. Yet the impact for Google was long-lasting.

And when we look at the mental health crisis that pervades both our workplaces and our homes, what do we see? The fixes we are attempting to apply – the mental health days, the wellness weeks, the mindfulness courses, the on-site therapy sessions, the hybrid working – all focus on how we can make the individuals who work for us feel better in isolation.

And yet – unsurprisingly – they don't.

If we take a step back and look at these issues not from the point of view of the issues themselves, but from what might be causing them, we can see that they all stem from the same deep, underlying problem. When we see ourselves in isolation from each other and our relationships, we miss a vital piece of the jigsaw – because what an individual experiences isn't a result of what is happening in their brain or even in the brain of the other person. It is what is happening *between the two.*

It is this 'relationality' that is at the core of each of these issues. In other words, the relationship between us affects the narratives we create about ourselves and others even more than the thoughts, feelings, and responses we have on an individual level. It's as if there are three people in every interaction: you, me, and the relationship itself.

When we think of relationality as a 'third person', it helps us understand why the solutions companies have used to combat workplace conflict are never going to work. As a psychotherapist, I can treat you and I can treat your colleague, but if I don't treat the way you relate to each other, I am treating the symptoms rather than the cause.

This cause – of the mental health crisis, poor workplace relationships, spiralling recruitment costs, low productivity – is what I call relational poverty. At first it might seem odd to suggest that we are relationally poor. Aren't we, after all, more connected than ever? Technology has allowed us to work in teams of hundreds rather than tens, to connect across time zones, to spend more time at home, to 'dial in' whenever we need to. And yet, there has never been a time in history when we were so relationally poor. Although we are hyperconnected, our biological need for connection is not being satisfied. Our interactions are functional, but not life-affirming; we are in touch, but not in relationship.

We have spent so much time thinking about the 'me' and the 'you' that we've forgotten about the 'us'.

A CHANGING WORLD

On 29 June 2007, twenty-seven-year-old Ryan O'Donnell stood in line outside Apple's San Francisco store. Six hours later, after battling sunburn, exhaustion, and a very full bladder, Ryan finally got his hands on what he had come for: the first iPhone.

Although Ryan already had a 'smartphone' – a Samsung BlackJack that could (just about) connect to Outlook – this was different. The iPhone had a responsive touchscreen, uninterrupted internet access, an in-built iPod. It would change *everything*.

And change everything it did. The iPhone made internet access ubiquitous. It allowed us to stay connected at all times. It offered a seamless mobile browsing experience. It also enabled the expansion of social media, with platforms like Facebook, Twitter, and, later, Instagram accessible no longer just from an iPad on the sofa at home, but on the bus, in the supermarket queue, at the petrol station. People started to share and consume content everywhere, *anywhere*, more regularly, more concisely – and more self-consciously.

The iPhone's App Store, launched the following year, introduced something else that was new: a vast ecosystem of third-party applications that allowed us to customise our devices to our own needs. We could listen to our own music, watch our own videos, play our own games. Our phones became an extension of our identities, curated to our tastes and experiences, as personalised as a fingerprint.

The smartphone is a 'me' device. Although it opens us up to a vast world of information, its primary job is to focus on its user. On FaceTime we can still see ourselves on-screen – a thumbnail reminder of our existences. We only have to ask Siri, and our personal assistant is all ears. Our phones are obsessed with pleasing us, listening to us, causing us to introspect: 'How are you feeling?', 'What do you like?', 'How can I entertain you today?'

Yet, at the same time as focusing on our individuality, technology limits our chances to connect. Zoom allows us to speak to our colleagues, but it removes the level of interaction we get when we meet face to face. Even our taxis are already paid for online, removing the need to speak to the driver beyond a departing 'Thank you'.

Of course, it's easy to blame the rise of technology for our connected-but-not-connected world. And technology is also a force for good. It allows us to be more productive, more efficient, more collaborative. But at what cost? We are only starting to see and understand the physiological changes that occur when human interaction is filtered through technology. How can we navigate its benefits while retaining our ability to connect?

WHY GENERATIONS STRUGGLE TO HEAR EACH OTHER

Of course, it wasn't surprising that Ryan O'Donnell wanted the latest smartphone. Millennials have grown up with technology at their fingertips. This is even more true for the generation that followed them: Gen Z, born between 1997 and 2012. These are the digital natives – those who have never known a world without social media. For them, the internet means they have access to the worst news about our planet – stories about terrorism, murder, theft, and violence – 24/7. Added to this, these anxiety-inducing stories are juxtaposed, almost instantaneously, with content meant to make them laugh. Threats of war one minute, funny cat videos the next.

Their interpretation of whether they are safe, whether society is safe, and what is expected of them in the world they live in, is based not on reality but on snapshots of the world curated by an algorithm. This means they have limited ability to tolerate real-life distress, so they become anxious, handing over their locus of control to others. They spend more time in fantasyland than any generation before them, but at the same time cannot get away from real life, as the interactions they have online never go away.

This bombardment with technology causes not only overwhelm, but an inability to concentrate and be truly present. It inhibits curiosity and critical thinking, and reduces the ability to develop adult discipline, connect on a face-to-face level, and ride the wave of feelings of fear or anxiety. As a result, the adolescent phase of human development now lasts much longer. And yet, by their early twenties, these digital natives are expected to leave education, enter the workforce, and become competent members of the adult world.

So how has the emergence of this generation into the workplace affected those already in it? Well, if the technological revolution led by the smartphone and AI looks like the biggest change in society in the last thirty years, the other seismic shift is this: the presence of three, four, even five generations in one workplace. Differences between generations are nothing new, of course – one generation always overtakes another with some friction

– but never has this been happening at such a rate and in such numbers.

Once again, it would be easy to take a side. We might attribute Gen Z's failure to launch to them being the 'snowflake' generation – tensions in the workplace are caused simply by their lack of resilience. But can you demonise a whole generation? After all, their challenges are real. They have agency but anxiety, are alone but never alone, have few dramatic experiences yet feel so much drama, live in both the authentic and the artificial world, are cognitively advanced but emotionally and psychologically behind. They lose their sense of innocence and trust earlier than any other generation before them.

And, of course, members of Gen Z have many positives: they innovate far more quickly than other generations, are tech-savvy, intuitively create new approaches, don't accept hierarchical or non-inclusive environments, care about their relationships, and are entrepreneurial. So who is at fault? Gen Z for the way they are, or millennials and Generation X for the way they raised them?

Or could what we are seeing be less about the failures of a single generation and more about the failure of generations to relate to each other?

The traditional approach to human resources in organisations is focused on the individual. Leadership programmes are about understanding yourself. Training is about personality types. One-to-ones identify strengths and weaknesses. The paradigm is focused on the 'I'. Yet again, when we look at this as human beings who need to connect, we see that the reason the workplace has become a more demanding place to be is not because *people* have become more demanding. It's because we've lost our ability to relate to our colleagues.

WHEN THE PACE OF CHANGE OUTRUNS OUR CAPACITY

In the last fifty years, the workplace has changed beyond recognition. But isn't that normal? After all, the one certainty about life is that it doesn't stay the same. But perhaps change is happening at an increased rate. Perhaps that's why it feels unmanageable.

One thing is clear: leaders are feeling an overwhelming sense of pressure as policies and structures become outdated before they've even had a chance to adjust. The result is burnout, decision fatigue, and absence due to stress and anxiety. At the same time as our need for adaptability is increasing due to changes like the emergence of AI and tech, generational tensions, and policies such as diversity and inclusion, our capacity to adapt seems to be decreasing. We are in the midst of an anxiety epidemic we just don't know how to solve. Generations see the differences between each other, not the opportunities for meaningful interaction and collaboration that those differences present. Our use of AI and tech focuses on productivity and flexibility for the individual, but ignores the fact that organisations are greater than the sum of their parts. Our responses to change depend on curiosity, adaptability, collaboration, and regulation, yet we ignore the relationships that would enable these things to happen. Perhaps it's not the challenges we face that need to change, but our approach.

For the last fifty years or so, there has been a shift in how we view the people in our organisations. They are no longer workers, but assets. Individually, they are soldiers in the fight for a productive and purposeful workplace. But this fails to understand that, as well as the two people in the conversation, we have a third asset: the relationships between us. The reason these issues threaten to engulf us is not because they are unmanageable, but because we are operating as individuals instead of as relational beings.

WE DO MORE THAN THINK - WE FEEL, SENSE AND RELATE

Some of the most powerful words I ever heard in the context of my work as a psychotherapist were said by one of my teachers, Hedy Schleifer: 'When in doubt, be relational.' It took me years to fully understand what these words meant. In fact, it was these five words that drove me to shift my work from the individual to the relational. I'll show you what I mean.

These words invited me to explore an idea I intellectually knew very little about yet which, deep down in my soul, made sense to me: that there is something else beyond the 'you' and the 'me' in a relationship – there is a space between. And that space doesn't just exist. It influences us both.

In the following years of research, I came to understand how relationships, and our experiences of relationships, shape our brains. They inform everything we say or do, because we don't operate in a vacuum. Whether we like it or not, our relationships with others, in conversation and interaction, are not only created by the interaction, but inform the interaction itself.

Until this point, the primary focus of my work had been individual psychology and the unconscious mind, and in particular the importance of childhood experiences and how they shape an individual's behaviour and mental health. This was filtered through the Freudian model, which says that the self is comprised of the **id**, the most primal part of the self; the **ego**, the rational, conscious part of the mind; and the **superego**, the internalised voice of authority and conscience. I believed the mental wellbeing of my clients was deeply rooted in their internal worlds – battlegrounds where these three forces contend for control.

This is the way we've traditionally looked at humans in psychology: as individuals separate from one another. It began with the ancient Greek philosophers, like Aristotle and Socrates, who emphasised the importance of individual autonomy and self-development. When Isaac Newton then described how everything is made of separate atoms which have no intrinsic connection to each other, it backed up the theory. This thinking still influences how we manage ourselves. We believe that, in order to be happy and fulfilled, we must somehow 'fix' the workings of our minds.

Then, among many others in the fields of psychotherapy, philosophy, and neuroscience, I read Thomas Fuchs, a German philosopher and psychiatrist. Fuchs offered a different view of the brain. He believed that, far from being a self-contained, computational machine, the brain is a facilitator of embodied, relational experiences. We are relational beings, and the brain is a relational organ.[4] In other words, we don't produce thoughts and feelings in isolation, but rather the brain is deeply embedded in the body and the world around it. We operate through ongoing interactions with our environment and relationships. It's who we are. Rather than being an organ in isolation, he said, the brain *participates* in relationships, so brains and relationships are not separate entities but intricately connected. Our interactions themselves actively influence how our brains develop and function.

Then I read Erik Erikson, a German-American developmental psychologist and psychoanalyst. He said the same thing, but added that we have eight stages of psychosocial development which happen at specific ages and are fundamental to how individuals grow. For example, between birth and eighteen months a child goes through a trust-versus-mistrust stage, developing and responding to its interactions with its caregiver, and this has a direct effect on its sense of security later in life. Crucially, each stage represents a critical conflict or challenge that's caused not by us, but by our relationships with our environment, in particular our social interactions. This agrees with Fuchs's argument that our human experience, including our mental development, is not just brain-based but deeply rooted in our social and environmental relationships.

I went further, reading about Porges' Polyvagal Theory, which shows how the vagal nerve and its regulation of the central nervous system is intricately linked to how we engage with others. In other words, our physical responses to safety or threat affect our emotions and behaviour. All of this was to say that the brain doesn't function in isolation but rather in a *relational* context, and that our functioning isn't just internally created, but co-created in relationship with others. Yes, the brain mediates these interactions, but it is the quality and dynamics of the relationship that shape our development.

As a therapist, I came to see that human beings are not individuals who relate to one another from a place of isolation, but that the relating itself influences us. This understanding changed the way I worked with people – whether they were individuals, CEOs, couples, families, or teams.

But I also learnt something as a human. After years of feeling unregulated, disassociated, and trapped in my emotional and sensate world, I learnt that there is a social and emotional space where we meet each other, and when we meet there, we can have healthy, effective relationships.

That space is our life's work as we continually shape and mould it from birth to old age. Most importantly, it shapes and moulds us, too.

For me, this changed everything. I realised that in order to treat the output of poor mental health – the epidemic we are seeing of stress, anxiety, depression, declining productivity and attention – we had to treat the *input*: the way we relate to one another.

We just have to learn how.

THE SPACE BETWEEN

In December 1999, just as the world was preparing for the millennium bug to potentially disrupt calendar data on computers across the globe, the pop star David Bowie gave an interview to *Newsnight*. Reporters titled it 'Internet is the new rock and roll'. Bowie described how the world was on the cusp of something both exhilarating and terrifying, something that would crash our ideas of content and how we consume it forever, something that for the first time would allow artist and audience to connect in real time. The internet, he said, was about to change everything.

'But it's just a tool, isn't it?' said Jeremy Paxman provocatively.

'No,' said Bowie, smiling but serious. 'It's an alien life form.'

What did Bowie mean? I think what he was talking about with such frightening accuracy was not the internet itself, but the tool as a reflection of our desire to connect. This was a key idea for Bowie. He believed that the interplay between art and artist was part of the art itself – an echo of the ideas of the French-American artist Marcel Duchamp at the start of the twentieth century.

He believed that art was not simply viewed with the eyes, but was fluid, surreal – an invisible interface between one person and another. In this way, the internet, Bowie said, was about to shift the power from creator to audience: 'What the piece of art is about is the grey space in the middle,' he said. '[And] that... space... is what the twenty-first century is going to be about.'[5]

You'll have realised that this idea isn't just about art. Just as Bowie and Duchamp saw their work not as static but as something that could be co-created with its audience, our experiences in life are not in isolation. Our interactions and conversations are not based merely on how we hear and see things, but on the invisible interface between us and each other – the space between.

So what *is* this space, and what can we do there?

When we shift our focus to what is going on between us rather than just what's happening on the inside, what we start to see is *possibility.* After all, each interaction we have has the potential for many different outcomes depending on the combination of the individuals. It isn't until that interaction occurs that the almost infinite number of possibilities becomes one outcome: connection or conflict, curiosity or dogma, regulation or dysregulation. All of this depends not only on what is happening for each participant, but on what happens in the space they co-create between them. This is why human relationships are so difficult, but also why they're so rewarding.

Most importantly, it's the quality of our interaction in that space that determines how we remember it. Was it joyful and alive? Or painful and antagonistic? Did we connect with the other person or find ourselves disconnecting? Although our brains belong to us and us only, they are only one part of the jigsaw. We are born in relationship, live in relationship, are challenged in relationship, and, ultimately, transform ourselves in relationship. The source of our disconnection isn't inside us, but in the space *between us*. How difficult would it be to step out of our isolated selves and focus on this space? What would happen if we did?

The thirteenth-century Persian poet Rumi said, 'Out beyond ideas of wrongdoing and rightdoing, / There is a field. I'll meet you there.' The poem is well known and well used, and I think it helps us to understand ideas of the space between us on a more practical level. In a world where the emphasis is always on the you and the me (and, let's face it, mainly on the me), it helps us to remember that there is a third entity: a space between us where right and wrong doesn't exist. More than that, this space is where the real business of life happens – because when we step away from our own perspective and the perspective of the other, we can see that between us there is something else entirely. Something that is worthy of our attention. The relationship between us is as important as the person either side of it.

It is in nurturing this space – the place beyond right and wrong, you and me – that we find our purpose. And rather than being something that sounds spiritual or 'woo-woo', this is something that is highly practical – in personal, psychological, societal and organisational terms. It shows us how to live, work, and interact in our organisations and teams in a way that makes us happier, more productive, more efficient, more psychologically safe, more innovative, and, ultimately, more employable.

Think about the last time you had a conversation, meeting, or review. How much time did you spend considering how *you* felt? Most of us reflect a lot on our own responses: on what we want to say next, on how to be heard, on how we feel about the other person in the room. If you are an empathic kind of person, perhaps you spent more time thinking about the feelings of other people: *What does she think of me? How did I come across? Is he angry? Bored? Irritated? Have I offended her with what I said?* Whether our focus is on what is happening for us or on what is happening for the other, we have created this narrative purely from an individualistic point of view. For this reason, our experiences at work – in our teams, boardrooms, and organisations – are driven entirely by our view that there is me and there is you and there is nothing in between.

But I have another question. Have you ever stopped to think that there is another point of reference – in addition to your own and that of your colleague – that exists alongside both of your individual responses? Because there is. In fact, in every conversation you have at work, formally or casually, with a teammate or a customer, you are creating something that didn't exist before.

The effect of that conversation.

Paying attention to this – the quality of the way we relate to each other – is what this book is about. It helps us explore how it is relationships – not just individuals – that drive what happens in the modern workplace, and at home. But most importantly, it shows that how we relate to each other is the key to understanding the challenges faced by organisations today.

WHY RELATIONAL WEALTH MATTERS

In 2012, over a decade before the 2023 redundancies, Google asked a researcher called Julia Rozovsky to conduct an experiment to understand what made teams the most productive. By identifying the conditions or dynamics that made teams succeed, they hoped to improve overall performance across the organisation.

Project Aristotle, as it was known, gathered data from over 180 teams. The researchers analysed the individual strengths of employees in those teams alongside how the teams worked together. Rozovsky and her team fully expected the results to show that productive teams relied on getting the best people – that the intelligence, experience, and expertise of their members were the key to their success. However, as they analysed the data, the researchers realised that the calibre of employee on the team didn't matter as much as they had thought. What mattered was how the team related to each other.

At the end of the experiment, Rozovsky concluded that it was in fact the presence of psychological safety – people's ability to be themselves, voice their opinions, ask questions, and admit mistakes – that was the most important factor in a team's success. Psychological safety meant that the team members were more willing to share ideas, more comfortable taking risks, more likely to manage conflict, and less likely to believe they'd be punished for making a mistake. In other words, it wasn't the individuals on the team that mattered, but the way the team co-created a relationship of trust.

Project Aristotle shows that relationships aren't a secondary issue at work, relegated to 'soft skills' and unrelated to economic output. Rather, the opposite is true: relationships are central to organisational success. Taking the focus away from the individual and putting it onto the relational makes us more creative, more productive, and higher performing. When employees feel connected and valued, they are more engaged, more resilient, and more innovative.

If we understand that our *relational* wellbeing is the source of our mental and emotional wellbeing rather than the other way around, we realise that by improving the way we relate to one another, we'll naturally improve the way we operate.

In the cases of Jill, the redundancies at Google, and our global mental health epidemic, we can now see that the source of disconnection isn't something intrinsically 'wrong' with each of the people involved, but an inability to relate to each other in the space between.

For Jill, her disconnection from her colleagues came from a place of fear of not being heard. The less she felt heard, the more she felt she had to speak. At Google, the disconnection felt by the employees wasn't a result just of being made redundant, but of their objectification by the company leaders as they failed to pay attention to the relational space. In other words, while on an individual level the redundancy was disappointing, *relationally* it felt counter to everything Google stood for.

As the global mental health epidemic becomes more of a focus, the solutions organisations are turning to rely solely on healing the individual. But this often means removing them from the environment they find challenging rather than creating an environment where they can thrive. Our efforts to provide mental health days, therapy sessions, and wellness weeks send the message that the individual can't cope. But what if we put the focus on regulating our feelings, encouraging open communication, valuing emotional intelligence, and creating opportunities for meaningful connection between employees instead? Would diversity and inclusion become less about employing a certain number of people representative of different sexes, cultures, or races and more about co-creating a space where we relate to each other? Would 'company culture' stop being about the *content* of what we do and say and the policies we might adopt, and start being more about the process of our conversations and interactions? What would happen to our organisations if they became places where people could truly relate to each other? Does this seem impossible?

On the eve of the millennium, David Bowie predicted that the twenty-first century would be about the 'grey space' – the uninhabited common ground between one person and another. I think he was right. If we come to understand that it is through relationship that we change, then suddenly a whole new way of looking at the workplace, and individual mental wellbeing, comes into play. Because if we were to take away, just for a moment, our desire to be right, to be first, to be loudest, to get across the content of our conversations, and instead focus on the process of what is *happening* in those conversations – not on what is being said, but on what is happening for us both when we say it – we could find the true relationship in our teams, our organisations, our families, and our society.

It would change *everything.*

CHAPTER 2

SURVIVAL MODE

"The human brain is hardwired with the belief that if we don't belong – if we do not feel secure and valued within our communities – our very lives are in peril."

HOW WE LOSE EACH OTHER

The moment of realising the vast implications of our ability – or inability – to relate to each other happened in an unlikely place.

It was 2012, and I was sitting in the hairdresser's, foils on my head, reading a magazine. Suddenly, in the mirror behind me I saw a young woman enter the salon. I could see instantly that she was unhappy, even distraught. I watched as she marched straight up to the receptionist and said in a loud voice, 'You've destroyed my hair.'

Even in reverse, I could see the mild panic in the receptionist's eyes. She quickly walked over to the other side of the salon, where the owner, Carl, was cutting someone's hair. She whispered in his ear, tilting her head to gesture at the young woman at the desk. Even from where I was sitting, I could see Carl's face fall. Together, they went over to the young woman and, steeling himself, Carl asked politely, 'Is everything OK?'

The woman turned to him and simply repeated what she'd said to the receptionist: 'You've destroyed my hair.'

Then she went on. 'I had highlights here last week and since then my hair has been breaking off in clumps. Look at it – there's hardly any of it left. It's absolutely ruined.'

What ensued was a charged, and very familiar, conversation. Carl began to tell the woman in no uncertain terms that he had *not* destroyed her hair and that he had always used that brand of highlights with no problem whatsoever. It simply couldn't have been caused by his treatment. Perhaps the woman herself had done something to cause the breakage?

At this the young woman became even more irate. She certainly had *not* ruined her own hair; it had in fact been in perfect condition before she'd come to the salon.

On and on it went. In the mirror, my eyes were now darting from one person to the other, watching as both became more and more upset and angry. I could see that there was an ever-decreasing chance this issue was going to be resolved. Knowing Carl quite well, I took a risk: I decided to intervene.

I got up, my cape still round my shoulders and my head still in foils, and I walked over to Carl and the young woman. 'Carl,' I said gently and with respect. 'You know how much I value you and what you do. I've been watching what's happening and I can see that this conversation is challenging for both of you. Would you mind if I found out a bit more about what's happening? Would that be OK?'

Carl nodded. I turned to the young woman and invited her to sit with me on the sofa. 'I could hear that you're really unhappy with your hair,' I said. 'Can you tell me what happened and what you're looking for?'

'Pardon?' she said.

'Could you tell me,' I repeated gently, 'what happened and what you need?'

Exasperated, she pointed at Carl. 'He destroyed my hair.'

'I've been hearing that,' I said. 'What happened? Can you tell me?'

At this she thought for a moment. Then she said, 'I'm a nanny. I saved up all year to come and have my hair done, and I came in here hoping to feel good about myself. Instead, my hair has been breaking off and looks worse than it did before. It's ruined.'

I nodded. 'And what's the one thing you want Carl to hear right now?'

She paused. Then the tears started to flow. 'I feel ugly,' she said.

I nodded. 'Carl,' I said, turning to the salon owner, 'what's happening for you as you hear that?'

Carl looked from me to the woman and back again. He said nothing. Then he walked over to the young woman and knelt down beside her. 'Come here,' he said gently, 'we're going to make this better.'

LISTENING WITHOUT HEARING

What I saw that day at the hairdresser's was the transformational power of paying attention to what is happening for each person in an interaction and in the space between. Both Carl and the young woman were experiencing something horrible happening inside them. For each of them, the need to defend and protect themselves was real and valid. But it was only when they stepped out of that experience and into the space between them that one could truly understand the other. Suddenly they weren't arguing anymore; they were *relating*.

This argument is the kind of exchange you might witness in any organisation or team. Blame over a failed project, a misunderstanding between colleagues, someone taking credit for another's idea – the topic is irrelevant. Something happens on a deep, cellular level that affects the two people involved and makes it virtually impossible to reconcile the conflict. I want to show you what that is.

When that young woman confronted Carl with her ruined hair, she was feeling distraught, angry, and let down.

On Carl's part, he felt defensive, 'got at', and afraid. But what was interesting to me is that underneath the feelings of anger, blame, and defensiveness, the systems of both individuals were trying to do the exact same thing.

They were trying to survive.

When you witness two people in a state of survival, one thing becomes clear. It doesn't matter what either party says or how reasonable – or unreasonable – they try to be. In fact, the two people in the conversation might just as well be speaking a different language, because they simply cannot understand the other's point of view. This is because while each person is so engrossed in their own experience of threat, they are almost *biologically* incapable of relating to the other. In other words, such is their need to survive that all other function and communication simply disappears.

Survival mode is the most primal state of our existence. It occurs when the risk of threat – real or perceived – causes us to react physiologically to preserve our safety. When we are in it, we cannot do anything else. We cannot hear what the other is saying to us, because we can pay attention *only* to our own need to survive. It's a response that is visceral, biological, and entirely subconscious.

Like all living creatures, humans have a strong system of response. From the minute we come into the world, we are looking out for danger – every second, every hour, every day of our lives. This is called neuroception. We are not aware of it, because it operates entirely beneath our conscious minds.

And we don't rely just on external factors to see where we are in danger. We also look internally, scanning our billions of data files of past experiences to match what is happening right now with what has happened in the past. The context of that memory is irrelevant – we just need to match a previous threat with the one we perceive today.

What our systems are looking for is information that can tell them how to behave in order to feel safe. Should I fight? Run away? Or do nothing, hoping that the threat will disappear on its own?

The response you default to is unique to you. You might find yourself defending your position, communicating aggressively, acting confrontationally, or arguing back. You might adopt a position of attack: you versus me, right versus wrong, my way or your way. This 'fight' mode is a heightened state of arousal. It means you narrow your focus and attention, making it almost impossible to truly engage with the other person's ideas or concerns. You fail to process information accurately – even if it is valuable feedback. After all, you are fighting for your life.

Alternatively, you might find yourself wanting to retreat. This 'flight' response is the system's way of saying, *I have to get away from this – now, immediately.* In flight mode, you would avoid confrontation, withdraw socially, or even walk out of a conversation entirely.

Both of these responses come from your sympathetic nervous system, the part of your autonomic nervous system that is activated by threat. It happens in organisations all the time. Imagine you are in a meeting and a manager asks an employee for an update on the work they've been doing for a specific project. In the past, this type of request has ended in criticism for that employee, so their system immediately perceives a threat. It knows that this situation is likely to end in them not feeling good enough, so it responds with a physiological reaction. Their heart rate increases, they start to sweat, they get a feeling of sickness in their stomach, their breathing quickens. All this happens so quickly and involuntarily that before they've even mentally processed the information the manager is asking for, they are in full-blown survival mode.

The impact on the space between those two people is instantaneous. The employee goes into fight mode. They become defensive, telling the manager that they haven't made as much progress as they'd like because their team hasn't provided the right information. When they do, they'll be able to complete their part of the work, but they don't see that happening any time soon, because half of the team aren't as competent as they should be. And by the way, they have concerns about a particular colleague that they've been meaning to raise...

Or the employee's response might be to flee. In this scenario, they might mumble something incomprehensible about the information being at their desk and they'll have to update the manager later, but they might not have time because they've been so busy. They're really sorry, they know they're being unprofessional, but they've just got so much on right now that they don't feel able to cope...

There is also another response, usually activated when neither fight nor flight has worked in the past. This is the dorsal state – the 'freeze' response activated by the ineffectiveness of the fight or flight response. Perhaps that employee was already in flight mode before the meeting started, doing their best to go under the radar, to stay quiet in meetings, to not be noticed, to become 'wallpaper'. Or perhaps they were already in a survival state of fight: their hackles raised by previous criticism, defences armed and at the ready. When their system now perceives this new potential threat to their competence and value, it knows it won't survive by fight or flight. So it does something else: it shuts down. This freeze response causes them to feel disconnected from their body, removed from the other people in the room and the task at hand. Their brain goes foggy, making it difficult to process any information relating to the meeting. They detach, dissociate, disengage.

What is the impact of this survival response on the space in the room? Perhaps the employee comes across as arrogant, failing to take responsibility, unable to accept or engage with feedback. Or maybe they seem disinterested, unresponsive, or aloof – a 'quiet quitter'. Their manager views them as offering so little to the discussion that it's clear they must not care. Perhaps they even think they are better than everyone else.

And just like that, in the blink of an eye, the space between those people has changed. By one or more of the participants entering a survival state, the space has turned from collaborative, safe, and dynamic to disjointed, fractured, and cold. The implications might even stretch further from this, creating politics in the team or a dysfunctional relationship between manager and employee. In time, if the situation isn't resolved, the employee might even be signed off sick or leave the company altogether.

Whatever the response looks like, survival mode is by nature a *dysregulated* state. This means that when you are in it, your system is using all its energy to help you survive the perceived threat. As a result, you are unable to relate to the person in front of you, to collaborate or problem-solve, because you are too busy surviving. This is what I saw that day in the hairdresser's: two people, in a professional setting, whose survival state made it *literally* impossible for them to relate to each other – because when you are in survival mode you cannot function in the way you need to in the space between. You cannot be truly present, you cannot hear what the other is saying, you cannot objectively reflect on your thoughts, you cannot be curious about what is happening for the other person. You cannot even care what you are both there to do.

There are three important points to remember about survival mode. First, these responses – whether fight, flight, or freeze – are not conscious. They are survival strategies activated by the nervous system to tell you that the situation is not safe. They are involuntary, automatic, and outside conscious choice.

Second, our survival mode responses are not mental. They are physical. In other words, *no thinking takes place.* This is because the system responds not in the brain, but in the body: the breath quickens, the heart rate increases, we sweat, shake, or feel sick. We might try to 'name' these emotions with words – anxiety, fear, anger, defensiveness – but what is happening in the body precedes this language.

Third, when we're in survival mode, it is fundamentally impossible to show up effectively in the space between. We are so involved in our need to self-preserve – to mitigate the risk around us, to survive the perceived threat – that we do not have the ability to occupy the space and relate to others. So, as we saw in the hairdresser's and in the project meeting above, our need to survive surpasses our need to relate to each other. In other words, in survival mode it's not that we don't listen – it's that we simply cannot hear.

WIRED FOR CONNECTION, STUCK IN SURVIVAL

In itself, this autonomic nervous system response isn't a bad thing: in moments of danger, it is invaluable as a mechanism for survival. But it has an impact on our ability to relate to those around us. For Carl and his customer, their survival mode responses meant that the space between them had become dangerous, preventing them both from showing up there in the way they needed to solve the conflict. The result was a familiar stress response, increased levels of cortisol and adrenaline, and an unresolved rupture in their encounter. In a perpetual downward spiral, the dysfunction in that space made both of their situations worse. As I'd learnt from my work as a therapist, humans are relational by nature. What I was witnessing was humans who are wired for connection stuck in a survival state where they could not connect. Their ability to show up in the space between was non-existent.

At that time, my experience as a therapist had been working with individuals or couples. I would help them to understand and show up in the space between them, working not only on their own emotional regulation but on the 'co-regulation' they needed to do with others. It worked. Time and time again, I could see people learning to direct their attention to the place where they interact, rather than just their own experiences and thoughts. That this was the solution to our mental health epidemic was not a theory, but, for me, a fact. I had never been more convinced of anything in my life.

But I suddenly realised what the implications of this scenario would be if it was played out on a bigger scale. Our failure to relate to others – this relational poverty I was witnessing – was not just a personal problem. It was happening everywhere: in our homes, our offices, our factories, and our shops.

In truth, this was obvious – organisations are, after all, systems made up entirely of people. And just like people, when organisations are in a state of survival, they find a way to protect themselves. By acting out of fear – the nervous system's response to the threats in the world around it – they become oblivious of the implications of their stance. Remember: these behaviours are not a choice – they are inevitable. Organisations, like individuals, are stuck in survival mode because of the response they have learnt to create. This causes conflict, disconnection, micromanagement, and blame when what they crave is innovation, reciprocity, communication, and collaboration. They avoid situations where they perceive risk and stay constantly on alert, always waiting for a threat to materialise in case they need to respond. As a result, we have workplaces where, instead of relating, people have learnt to avoid, to mitigate, and to protect.

That day, I realised what the implications of relational poverty were – for our individual mental health and for the workplace. I realised that for organisations, relationships weren't just an aspect of 'culture' they needed to pay attention to. They were the single biggest threat to their existence.

If you look, you can see dysregulation everywhere in the workplace. Managers on the back foot, waiting for a complaint or an underperformance; employees afraid to fail, because they lack psychological safety; leaders struggling to show empathy; teams and departments poisoned by miscommunication; poor self-awareness, competitiveness, inauthenticity, defensiveness, black-and-white thinking, and a lack of belonging – all because of our failure to regulate our nervous systems enough to step into the space between.

The challenges of the new workforce I've described create the perfect conditions for survival mode relationships. The emergence of technology, the generational divide, the ever-increasing speed of change – all around us are risks we're trying to mitigate by creating certainty. But at the same time, as organisations we seek outcomes that can result only from co-regulation: creativity, novelty, ownership, and innovation. That's the contradiction. What we need as humans – belonging, connection, acceptance, and safety – and what we need as organisations – innovation, curiosity, collaboration, and productivity – cannot be separated into component and system. The experience we create in the space between matters not only to the cogs, but to the machine itself.

The result is organisations that survive but don't thrive. We have presenteeism but not presence, 'culture' but not curiosity, reaction but not reflection, criticism but not candour, a collective role but not a collective purpose, strategy but not solidarity, diversity but not delight in difference, anxiety but not vulnerability. And it all stems from our desire to preserve at all costs the safety we perceive in being positional, rather than surrendering to the vulnerability of discovering what's happening for us and the people around us.

We are relational by nature. Yet we have somehow moved to a place where not only are we unable to relate to others, but we are not even paying attention to what's happening for *us*. Our organisations, just like us, are in survival mode, with people not unwilling to listen, but unable to hear. The result, I realised that day at the hairdresser's, is that nothing will change on a global scale until we are willing to address what happens in that space between – individually, collectively, organisationally, universally.

I had to get out of the therapy room and into the office.

WHAT I MEAN BY RELATIONAL CAPACITY

Increasing our ability to relate to each other on an individual and organisational level seemed like a big ask. Everywhere I looked, workplaces had no real solution to the relational poverty that was rife. Managers would hire culture executives and HR advisors and change consultants and mental health practitioners, but none of these solutions worked in the long term.

I saw this on a small scale when a middle manager from a large organisation came to me after three months of being signed off sick with stress. He was on anti-anxiety medication and had worked with a number of therapy professionals before finding his way to me. When I asked him to tell me what had led to him being signed off, he said that he had been put on an informal performance review and it had gone badly.

'I see,' I said. 'How did the performance review come about and what happened?'

'I have no idea,' he said. 'I'm a high performer – my team and I have exceeded our targets for the last two years.'

'So what were the areas they asked you to improve?' I asked.

'Well, they said I talked too much in meetings, gave too much detail, overwhelmed people with information, that sort of thing. I thought that was a bit rich, as I had always come up with helpful contributions. So I took steps to improve that.'

I nodded. 'Can you share how you have done that?'

'I don't say anything in meetings anymore,' he shrugged, 'unless I absolutely have to. I figured that if they don't like what I have to say, someone else can step up.'

I nodded. 'Anything else?'

'Yes,' he said. 'My line manager said that he feels I don't listen to what he says in my one-to-ones, and I don't follow through on actions. I was also reprimanded for an issue with a client that was escalated to senior management, but that was totally unfair and unfounded. It happened when I was off sick with Covid. It wasn't my fault. I started having panic attacks shortly after that. I was so worried I'd lose my job, but I really was trying my best.'

As I work in a multidisciplinary way, the next day I spoke to the man's GP. She told me that this was in fact the third time this patient had been signed off work in six years.

He had been on anti-anxiety medication for most of that time, and every time he returned to work the same thing happened. I reflected on this situation over the coming days. This client had been offered plenty of solutions – an HR response, a line management response, a medical response, and even a therapeutic response – but they had all failed.

Why?

The language this man was using showed me that his nervous system was about as activated as it gets. He was in survival mode and had demonstrated various of its responses to the threats around him. He had gone from fight – defending his position and blaming others – to flight – refusing to talk in meetings and ignoring action points – to dorsal state (freeze) – feeling hopeless, apathetic, and unable to cope, resulting in being signed off work.

What nobody in that organisation had done was deal with the real issue at hand: his need to regulate his emotional response and co-regulate with others to create solutions, connection, and growth, even in the conversations that were challenging. By removing himself from the situation, my client had not allowed himself to enter the space between him and his manager for long enough to find out what was truly happening there.

Let's think about it this way. If I want to increase the strength of a particular muscle, I need to put it under pressure. I need to test it through some form of resistance training so that microscopic tears in the muscle fibres initiate repair and recovery and make the muscle stronger. It's the same for our capacity to relate to each other. The psychologist Stephen Porges said, 'Our nervous system evolved in the context of relationship.' We need to subject our relationships to challenges that exceed their current capabilities so that we can learn from them and build stronger, healthier, and more effective connections. By removing ourselves from these encounters, we're refusing to use the very muscle we need to develop.

This is our 'relational capacity', and increasing it is our life's work. But how?

When Stephen Porges talks about the nervous system this way, he is talking about a capacity that goes beyond our autonomic responses. In fact, the nervous system has evolved further than the fight-flight-or-freeze response. Unlike some animals, we have a social engagement system, a biological instrument for social connection, called the vagus nerve. This major component of the nervous system enables social bonding by regulating the facial muscles, voice, and eye contact – the cues we use to signal safety and form connections with others. When we experience these cues positively, they suggest safety and calm, and we in turn can start to regulate our own social cues in response. In this way, the nervous system of one person can actually start to influence the nervous system of another so that we adapt our demeanour to help the other to feel safe. When this happens, even if the content of the conversation is difficult, we can regulate our survival state and start to relate to each other.

This is what Porges and others call 'co-regulation'. It's the process by which we mutually regulate each other's emotions and responses, attuning to what's happening for the other and providing support, comfort, and validation. It allows the other to feel understood, providing a sense of safety and trust. And it's born from reciprocity, allowing us both to step into the space between us where the magic of relationship truly happens.

An orchestra is made up of many musicians, all playing their individual parts. But each member of that orchestra cannot play just for themselves. They have to understand that they are but one part of the whole, and that all the other musicians are also playing.

And then there is the third entity, apart from the player and the musicians around them. It is the sum of their parts, the sound created when all the musicians play together. It is the orchestra itself.

We are all responsible for our own parts, our self-awareness, empathy, and communication, the noisy, isolated tune we play in the silence of our minds. But we are also responsible for the ensemble itself. We must pay attention to what the other musicians are playing, the space between what we play and what the other plays that is so vital to the functioning of us all. As part of this orchestra, we are not in charge of just our own pieces of music. We must accept accountability for the orchestra as well. As Isaac Stern said so beautifully, 'Music is what happens between the notes.'

DRIVING IN INDIA

Without connection to the relational space, we will struggle to discover the safety that can exist in our relationships. Dan Siegel, a leading interpersonal neurobiologist, says in his book *Brainstorm* that there are three elements to relational communication.[6] The first is what is happening inside you – we could call this insight. The second is what is happening inside another person – we could call this empathy. And the third is that all-important experience of what is happening in the space between.

We could call this communication, but I don't think that word goes far enough. Rather, it is our *relationality* – our capacity to connect in and co-create a safe space between us. This is where the magic of relationships happens, but to achieve this, we have to start taking responsibility for the space ourselves. If we don't, we use it as a dumping ground for our unspoken emotions – through a word, a look, a reaction, a withdrawal – and by doing so we pollute that space. When the space feels uncomfortable like this, we react to this discomfort in some way that makes it more uncomfortable, and the space becomes dangerous. The way we react is different – some of us will explode and get angry, others will constrict or withdraw their energy. But once two dysregulated reactions come together, the danger in the space grows, and before we know it, we are reacting together to a negative space we have co-created.

As organisations, as individuals, we are constantly trying to predict the dynamics of this space. What will the other do next? How will we keep ourselves safe? To do this, we create biases and barriers, positioning ourselves in a certain way to prevent infection from the other. And in doing so we fail further to reflect on what is happening. We don't think about our thinking, because we are too busy trying to avoid the threat.

While survival is something we do alone, relationship is something we can do only together – by regulating ourselves and co-regulating with others to create a space that is safe. I know why none of the solutions had worked for that manager who was signed off sick. By leaving work whenever he failed to relate to his colleagues, he was taking himself away from the only place of repair. The result was that he was stuck in a state of survival, unable to co-create a safe place to be with those around him, because he did not know how to step into the messiness of relationships.

Years ago, I had the pleasure of visiting India. While I was there, I noticed with horror the way the locals drove. There seemed to be no rules – no lines on the road, no signs telling everyone what to do, no system to keep everyone safe. But as I spent more time on the roads, I started to see that there *was* a system, it was just based on principles rather than rules. The drivers in India didn't see themselves as having one right of way or priority over another, but rather as being part of a collective flow. They had a way of treating other road users that meant they didn't need individual rules. They just existed, between and among, like vessels on a river moving up and down to where they needed to go. In all of it they were fully cognisant of others and had no intent to harm. The beeps of warning, the pauses, the squeals of brakes that I was hearing were all part of the endless flow of traffic that appeared messy but was in fact self-organising. It was the fullness and chaos of life – and it worked.

Driving in India is what is known as a complex system. Although it has no rules, it has emergent properties, processes that arise from the flow of the system's elements over time. In other words, it is self-organising. As time goes on, even without rules, a process emerges. Elements of the system turn back on themselves and regulate that from which they came, on and on, until a positive feedback loop reinforces itself. In this way, it is 'chaos-capable' – erratic and unpredictable, but also functioning in a perfect and effective way.

Dan Siegel says, 'The self is not defined by the boundaries of our skin.' I am not just 'me', I am 'we' – I have an integrated way of being in the world. That way of being has no road markings, but is rather a complex system – self-organising, messy, emergent. Chaos-capable. And in that messiness lies a capacity to co-create a system where we flow endlessly where we need to go, bumping into each other, yes, but also, more than simply surviving, learning from that impact, shaping and being shaped by those interactions.

Relational capacity – the measure of an individual's or a team's ability to regulate emotions, co-create solutions, cultivate connection, grow and thrive in the face of constant change – is not about managing emotions or controlling our impulses. It's about entering into the messy, dynamic dance of human interaction, where both self-regulation and co-regulation occur in a fluid, nuanced way. It demands that we step out of survival mode and develop a kind of non-anxious presence – one that is fully attuned to the other person's needs while at the same time being grounded enough to support our own. It requires practice, awareness, and a commitment to the co-creation of that space between – to building relationships that honour both ourselves and others.

We need to get comfortable with the uncomfortable, increasing our windows of tolerance for the ruptures that inevitably happen and knowing how to repair them in a way that makes the relationship stronger. This leads to greater resilience, adaptability, collaboration, and the ability to get things done.

Our relationships are born not by avoiding the messiness, but by understanding that messiness is the process by which they grow.

CHAPTER 3

OUR CAPACITY FOR CHANGE

"Our ability to change relies on us reaching not for the aspirin, but for the vitamin."

WHY THE PAST DOESN'T STAY IN THE PAST

'If our response to threat is automatic, how could we ever hope to change it?' That's a question I am asked a lot, both by individuals in my therapy room and by the organisations I now work with to bring about change. It's a valid question. If we are biologically programmed to respond to threat by activating survival mode, how can we possibly be expected to override that response?

Whenever I am asked that question, I think about an unusual kind of theatre.

A prisoner and a prison officer are seated across from one another in a room. Their positions are opposite: jailed and jailer; punished and punisher. Their lives have been shaped by systems that cast them as either adversary or enforcer, and each carries deep wounds – one from a life of struggle and reparation, the other from a career spent navigating danger and distrust.

One day, a group of actors comes into that prison and asks the inmates and the officers to perform an unusual task. They are to act out stories to each other from their personal experiences, but instead of each participant acting out their own narrative, they must tell it to the other in order for *them* to perform it. In other words, the roles will be reversed. The prisoner will enact the officer's story, while the officer will step into the prisoner's shoes. Through the medium of drama, each must express either the other's fear, loss of humanity, and need for control, or their pain of incarceration, disconnection, and despair.

This 'playback theatre' exercise between prisoners and prison officers actually happened, under the expert guidance of the Portland Institute for Loss and Transition. It allowed two people in an organisation to go beyond listening to each other and trying to understand each other's experience to truly connecting with it. In doing so, something remarkable happened. The emotional field between them shifted. The boundaries that had once separated them dissolved. And through this relational engagement a shared humanity emerged, offering the possibility of healing not just for the individuals in the workplace, but for the workplace itself.

OUR PAST VOTES LOUDLY IN OUR PRESENT

In a world where traditional mental health models are set up to make us feel like something is wrong with us, it's easy to miss the fact that everything we do or say has meaning. This is true whether it makes sense to us and those around us or not. Whether we fight, flee, or freeze – and the manner in which we do it – tells us less about the situation we are in and more about the place we came from to get there.

Have you ever stopped to think why someone in your organisation takes on that piece of work when they know they are already overloaded? Or why someone doesn't speak up in meetings but voices their complaints afterwards?

Have you ever wondered why a person always procrastinates, repeats themselves, or refuses to ask for help? Why would one person's instinct be to fight when another's is to flee?

The response we choose in survival mode is a product of the experiences we've had. If you remember, these are stored not in our brains, but in our beings, and they show us how we need to behave in order to survive. This is the autonomic nervous system responding to data it has already gathered and stored neatly in the cellular 'memories' we created from those experiences. It is then used to inform how we show up and interact in the here and now, influencing not just how we think, but how we respond.

Imagine if, as a child, I had a parent who criticised me often. Every day I might have heard some version of 'It's a shame you didn't score better in that test' or 'Why can't you keep your room tidy like I asked?' In other words, *What is wrong with you?*

Now imagine what happens when, as an adult, I am presented with a performance appraisal where I am given a list of areas I should improve. Even if these suggestions make sense in my brain, the *process* of this criticism is remembered in my system. *I've been here before*, it says. My system only has to reach into its embodied memory to find multiple examples of times when I had to justify myself to win back the affection of my parent. At work, this comes out as *I didn't do it wrong. It was someone else. It only happened because I wasn't here last week. No one told me. I couldn't possibly have been expected to know that. It's not my fault.*

This is my survival mode showing up as a desire to fight. My hackles are raised, my heart rate increases, my hands start to shake, and cortisol rushes through my body. Everything about my system tells me *I am in danger*. And so, I react defensively, taking the position that I did not mess up, someone else did. It's not my fault. And in that moment,

I can no longer hear the content of the conversation. My system is so busy trying to survive that I am no longer fully present, I cannot try to understand what is happening for the other person, and I certainly cannot understand what is happening in the space between us. It's as if I am deaf.

To my manager, this comes across as a different narrative, which they interpret as *She is arrogant, completely unable to accept criticism, acts in self-interest rather than the interest of the organisation.* But, of course, this narrative is made up. I am in fact a conscientious and dedicated employee. My own narrative is that my boss is micromanaging, highly critical, out to get me no matter what I do – which also, of course, is entirely made up. And somewhere, in the space between us, is the truth.

My response in this scenario is not because I am 'wrong', it is because I am me. One of my psychology peers once summed this up by saying, 'Our past votes silently in our present.' But I would go further. I'd say that our past votes *loudly* in our present. In fact, the system's response to threat is so powerful that everything we have ever experienced becomes formalised in meaning. In other words, we construct a narrative around it which then shows up in every interaction, every thought, and every response, both in the near and distant future. It happens for us, it happens for the other – and it affects everything that happens between us.

This is not to say that it all goes back to childhood and we can simply blame our parents for the way we are. That's the easy way out, although it is not easy for long. What it means is that our autonomic nervous systems are the product of the past – whether that was forty years ago or forty minutes ago. Our felt experiences in the past influence our felt experiences in the present because our memories of relational pain are intense. It doesn't matter what the present context of the interaction is, the memory of the experience is there.

This is why our responses today have little to do with the context in which we find ourselves, but *everything* to do with the way we've related to others in the past.

THE STILL FACE

In 1975, a mother sits in a white room. She is facing a baby – her baby – who is sitting in a bouncing chair. The woman smiles and talks to the baby, cooing and engaging with him as a mother does. But suddenly, her demeanour changes. She stops smiling and talking, or in fact responding to the baby at all. Her face becomes expressionless. The baby tries to get her attention again: he smiles, vocalises, even reaches out to her. Still she doesn't respond. Eventually, the baby becomes distressed, crying and arching his back, doing anything he can to get his mother to notice him. Finally, he stops crying and looks away, defeated.

This was the Still Face Experiment, a purposeful study led by psychologist Ed Tronick and designed to discover how a child's emotional attachment is affected by the level of its caregiver's engagement. It proved that even very young infants are sensitive to social cues and highly attuned to their caregivers' attention. What's more, they rely on these interactions to feel secure, not just now, but into adulthood. When the caregiver is emotionally unavailable (even momentarily), it creates stress and anxiety for the child. This represents a rupture in its social connection which, Tronick argued, will influence that child's attachment style in the long term. If a child's attempts to seek connection are consistently met with indifference or dismissal, for example, the child will learn to suppress its emotional needs into adulthood. This repeated lack of emotional attunement teaches the child that expressing emotions or seeking help is ineffective or unwelcome, so they develop a coping mechanism in the form of an avoidant attachment style. In organisations this shows up as unwillingness to participate, hesitation to provide ideas or opinions, or even apparent procrastination or poor time-management.

If the child has a caregiver who sometimes provides comfort, love, and attention but at other times is unresponsive, however, they would develop what's known as an anxious attachment style. This stems from them being unsure about whether their needs will be met, so they become preoccupied with gaining people's attention and approval. They worry about being rejected or unloved and are on high alert (hypervigilant) for signs of the withdrawal of attention. If they sense it, they will amplify their emotions, perhaps by crying, being clingy, or constantly seeking reassurance. At work, this might be the person who talks too much, repeats themselves, or takes on too much work in the desperate desire to prove their worth.

It is only people who are given comfort and connection, validated and supported to self-regulate their emotions, who develop an attachment style we would describe as secure.

Whether positive or negative, our experiences of how the ruptures in our relationships were dealt with stay with us. They are not intellectual memories, but physical ones – not cognitive, but felt in the body. The attachment style we subsequently develop is what we encounter whenever we go into survival mode. In other words, the physical symptoms our systems are confronted with are learnt as a response to threat, and it is around this 'embodied' experience that we create a narrative. This isn't necessarily verbalised, but rather becomes a felt experience that is held in our implicit memories. It is subjective, biased, and physiologically encoded, and, most importantly, it fails in one important task: our ability to take into account what is happening in the exact same way for the other and in the relational space.

This is why the playback theatre experienced by the prison officers and their inmates was so powerful. It was an opportunity to reflect on their felt experiences and to be curious about the felt experience of the other. Only then could they regulate their corresponding responses in order to meet in a place between. Just as the cause of survival mode is physiological, so is the solution. We must go back to the body, not to relive past ruptures, but to learn what is happening for us when we do.

THE MUSIC AND THE DANCE

When you understand where your survival mode response comes from, your behaviours make so much more sense. Not only that, but so do the behaviours of others. Our responses are the music we all dance to – both as individuals and as organisations. That board member who talks over everyone in meetings? The colleague who can't cope with feedback? The person who cannot meet deadlines? When you look at these behaviours through the lens of that person's style of attachment, the reason for them suddenly becomes clear. That's not to say that you'll know their childhood history, of course, but you can spot their attachment style through their behaviour. And when you take this as the meaning of their response instead of your own narrative – your made-up story of incompetence, self-interest, arrogance, or whatever it is you have written – you step out of the judgement of 'right' and 'wrong' altogether and step into the space between. This is where, regardless of the *content* of the conversation, you can finally see what is actually *happening*.

As a therapist, 'What is happening for you?' is one of the most powerful questions I ask. This is because this process – the understanding of our natural responses – isn't just about how someone *feels*, but the embodied experience they are having. What 'happens' for us in a particular situation is directly linked to the type of attachment we formed as children: secure, anxious, or avoidant. There is no right or wrong in these attachment styles – they are simply how we exist as a result of our felt experiences. It is only when we learn to understand these styles that we can work together to increase our relational capacity. This is the magic that occurs when we truly relate to one another – and it is co-created, co-influenced, and co-managed by our ability to understand who we are.

It's important to say that, by understanding, we are not seeking to override. In fact, the journey from survival mode to relational capacity isn't a transition from one way of functioning to another at all. It is a paradigm shift – a move away from an individual response to one of co-regulation. To get there, to find the flow in the dance of interaction between us, we must seek not to overrule our internalised responses, but rather to understand them and learn to regulate them.

This emotional regulation is not an act of self-control, neither is it an emotional or behavioural adjustment. In my work, I've seen how people often shut down or silence parts of their inner worlds that feel inconvenient or painful. This often suppresses the voice of the person within, wielding self-control like a hammer, rather than listening with curiosity and compassion. This type of self-regulation is just a temporary control – it reinforces disconnection rather than resolving it.

No, self-regulation is a developmental leap, a nuanced and relational process, like fanning the brakes on a car instead of slamming them. It enables us to adapt to the moment with flexibility and grace, creating space for a more 'meta' perspective where we see our reactions, assumptions, and emotions in relation to the broader field.

This is because true self-regulation is in service only of the relationship. It allows us to stay attuned to the other's experience without being overwhelmed by our own emotions, enabling us to remain present even in the face of someone else's distress. By doing so, we increase our capacity for providing empathic support and validation, which in turn allows the other to self-regulate, too.

This is the magic of acknowledging what is happening for us, for the other, and in the space between. It is what true co-regulation and relationship are made of. We are no longer locked in a zero-sum game of controlling or being controlled, but can engage in a subtle dance of interaction, where presence, empathy, and reflection give rise to deep and lasting change: the self-organising of a beautiful but complex system.

As I said before, this is more than an intellectual exercise. It requires what I call credulous thinking – a willingness to step into the logic and experience of the other person and to understand their perspective as if it were your own, even if you don't fully agree with it. In many ways, this is the opposite of critical thinking as it's traditionally taught. Critical thinking, particularly in Western education, often focuses on the power of argument and logic to dismantle an opposing viewpoint. As a result, we end up alone in our positions, defending our right to be right, rather than doing the deeper work of exploring how we can hold different truths and still find common ground.

Credulous thinking is the act of embracing the other's perspective. It demands empathy – the kind of understanding that goes beyond thoughts and feelings and discovers what's actually happening for the person in front of us. It's the kind of understanding that would allow you to act out the other's felt experience on a stage, because it now makes total sense to you – even if you don't like how it shows up.

THE ASPIRIN AND THE VITAMIN

What would it mean to shift from control to connection like this? To replace the automatic reflex of dominance with the curiosity of dialogue? To transform disconnection into growth and healing, not just on a personal level but in our organisations, too? How could it happen?

The work I do with organisations invites them to explore how to cultivate this relational capacity, not with rules, but with principles and values. It shows them how to move from a narrow, self-focused existence to one in which we can truly see and hear the other, and it shows them how this capacity can be used to correct our relationships with ourselves and our relationships with others.

We have all had felt experiences that affect the way we show up and respond today. But as adults we also have a responsibility for how we behave in the presence of perceived or real threat – whether we shout, run, blame, shame, criticise, or shut down. We must be accountable for expanding our ability to relate to other people. We can do this only through making meaning of our experiences and adopting principles that allow us to show up for and understand the felt experiences of others. This allows us not only to choose how we respond, but to have a corrective, positive felt experience in the here and now.

The challenge with organisational change – and the self-help industry as a whole – is that it tries to give us tools to help us fix ourselves. It goes into workplaces and asks change to happen on an individual level, expecting that change to improve the system of which it is a part. But in doing this, it fails to show how it is in relationship that we know ourselves. We need more. Our departments, teams, and companies need to value relationality in its own right, seeing it as central to our ability to adapt, thrive, and run more effective processes.

This is why the way organisations deal with change often doesn't work. They coach their leaders to develop new habits – compromises that attempt to override their internal responses – rather than dealing with why they responded that way in the first place. This leaves them with the *knowledge* of how to act, but not the true transformation that has to happen for them to 're-feel' their past experiences. It's like reaching for a solution, day after day, week after week, without stopping to treat the cause – which is our failure to understand what is happening for ourselves and others when we try to relate to each other. We can teach methods to collaborate better, but they will only ever be a treatment, not a cure. This is because we don't need an aspirin to numb the pain; we need a vitamin to prevent it.

I am a right-handed person, so I would instinctively and naturally catch a ball with my right hand. But if a sports coach told me that catching the ball with my *left* hand would drastically improve my performance, I would be willing to give it a go. In time, with practice and determination, I might even be able to learn this behaviour to the point that I could catch a ball with my left hand just as easily as my right.

But what if one day I were to open a door and, without warning, someone threw a ball at me? Which hand would

I use then? No matter how we have learnt to behave, when threatened we will always revert to our natural attachment styles and survival state. This is because coaching for habits is cerebral rather than felt, so when we take the 'thinking' part out of the equation (as we do in survival mode) we go straight back to our previous models. In times of perceived or real threat, it doesn't matter what you know – it matters only that the threat is there.

So how *do* we set up organisations to thrive? It's worth saying here that the disconnection, poor mental health, miscommunication, and lack of resilience we are experiencing in organisations today are not due to a lack of knowledge – we have, after all, been coached to within an inch of our lives. No, our disconnection is due to us not having had a felt experience that 'corrects' the one that caused our insecure attachment. The siloed nature of departments and organisations, the amount of time we spend meeting online instead of in person, our lack of psychological safety and constant mitigation of risk all create disconnection that puts us into a permanent state of survival. Over time, these ruptures-without-repair have left us intolerant of change, inflexible to difference, and terrified that something will come along to overwhelm us. The only way to get out of survival mode is to experience our responses again in a more regulated way.

How? By embracing the mess.

When we understand that relationships strengthen through the process of repair, we see that the way to increase our windows of tolerance is not to withdraw from the process but to embrace it. We have to be able to navigate the differences between us in such a way that, over time, small relational ruptures *expand* our capacity for empathy and psychological safety rather than damage it. We need to learn to hear each other – listening with our whole beings

– and to reflect on our experiences by self- and co-regulating. When we spend time together having one conversation and the right conversation, we get to truly understand each other and improve the quality of our relationships and our ability to navigate rupture and repair. This is the best predictor of health, both on an individual level and a corporate one.

Most organisations engage in transformation as if it were a mechanical process. They try to navigate the difference by implementing change: sequences of events they believe will lead from where they are now to an outcome they think they can envisage. But they fail to build the core relational capacity that helps us, as humans, navigate the journey between where we are and where we are going.

If we fail to build our relational capacity, nothing changes. In fact, only 16% of organisational transformation is successful. Why? Because it favours performance over principles. We are not machines, and neither are our organisations. We cannot be taught what to do, say, or think in order to fix our felt experiences. We are relational, emergent, self-organising – musicians playing individually but participating collectively.

This can happen only through a corrective, positive felt experience. To engage in it, we must understand and apply principles – not behaviours, but a transformational development in the way we relate to those around us. These principles cannot be learnt as a child learns by rote. They must be felt – experienced as they happen when we put ourselves in a position to accept them. When they are, our bodies learn a different way to be.

THE FOUNDATIONS FOR RELATIONAL CAPACITY

So what are these principles we can live by, and how can we employ them to gradually transform our interactions? The 'how' is what the rest of this book is about – the individual practices and processes that help us to embody these principles in our organisations. They are the foundation for creating in organisations the security and confidence we need to respond to the uncertainty we face with AI, the ever-changing needs of the workforce, and the increasingly diverse number of generations working together. There are eight, and they work together just as much as separately. The summaries here only scratch the surface – in the following chapters I will show you exactly how they can be applied and then embodied so they change our *experiences* of working together as much as our attitudes.

Presence

Presence allows us to be fully engaged and available in the current moment – to ourselves, to the other, and in the relational space. Practising being 'there', not just physically and mentally but relationally, helps us bring our attention, intention, and attunement to what is unfolding on a deeper level, creating a culture of psychological safety in our teams and organisations.

Reflection

Reflection is the process of opening the gap so we can 'think about our thinking'. It encourages self-awareness, understanding, empathy, growth, and change. It is both an individual and a collective practice, involving moments of personal introspection as well as shared dialogue to explore what's happening in you, me, and the space between. It allows us to form working relationships based on trust rather than opposition.

Curiosity

Curiosity is more than a fleeting interest in how the other is feeling. It's the spark that ignites empathy, the glue that binds disparate ideas, and the catalyst for innovation in our teams. It is letting someone or something else influence our thinking, allowing us to break down assumptions and biases. In organisations, it facilitates innovation and true collaboration.

Respectful candour

This is not an excuse to 'tell it how it is' – an attitude that can be harmful in organisations. It is constructive honesty, offered with positive intent, in service of the greater good of the team, project, or goal. Respectful candour is about a behaviour, not the person, and it requires us to remove absolutes – it is not about what someone 'always' does, but about what is happening for them now and the effect this has on the people around them.

Vulnerability

Vulnerability has the power to create trust, ignite creativity, and drive innovation. After all, how do I build trust with you if I don't know who you are? As well as intellectual acceptance, it requires the courage to act – to share, explore, and grow. Part of that might mean sitting with a non-answer or solution, or taking part wholeheartedly in the rupture-and-repair process. All this allows us to turn shared risk into shared success. It is the only way to build genuine human connection.

Navigating difference

Navigating difference isn't just about acknowledging diversity – it's about actively engaging with it to co-create, innovate, and drive collective success. It is about leveraging diverse thoughts, experiences, and perspectives, not only to coexist, but to succeed and thrive. It is bedded in the belief that the collective capabilities of an organisation or team exceed the sum of its individual contributors, and that we can build intentional practices that prevent resentful compromises and genuinely align diverse perspectives.

Being in service of a shared goal

Being in service is centred on one simple yet profound question: 'How can I help?' More than just about steering the ship, this question is about genuinely serving those who help it sail. Being 'in service' requires us to connect with and believe in something greater than ourselves – the project, team, or organisation itself. It demands that we do not avoid the difficult conversations, but rather face what we don't want to face in order to get things done.

A mindset of abundance

Unlike positive thinking, which generally focuses on maintaining an optimistic attitude, a mindset of abundance sees the work we do as filled with limitless opportunities and resources. This encourages us to act with generosity and creativity, going far beyond optimism. When individuals and teams embrace this mindset, they are more inclined to share resources, ideas, and energy. It is the precursor to psychological safety, leading to collaborative environments where challenges are seen as opportunities to grow, innovate, and connect.

Each of these principles is a transformation in itself. Learning how to embody and apply them, little by little, one conversation at a time, is at the core of self- and co-regulation. But the beauty is that each one is also inextricably interwoven with the others. So if we fail to reflect, we will struggle to be present; if we fail to be curious, we will not be able to reflect; if we fail to reveal vulnerability, we will never learn to navigate difference... and so on. Unless we can apply them – in both a cognitive way and an embodied, *felt* way – we will struggle to be the organisations we want to be, because our survival state and attachment styles will continue to get in the way of our ability to self-regulate and co-regulate in order to create cultures of belonging, empathy, psychological safety, and resilience.

This requires an element of risk. Without risk we cannot build psychological safety in the space between, we cannot establish a sense of belonging, explore and change our biases, step out of our comfort zones, challenge our beliefs and ideas, or let go of our need to be right. Without risk nothing will change.

In all of this we need self-awareness, empathy, reciprocity, and effective communication, but above all an understanding that someone else's thinking can influence our thinking without harming us. We need to grow the confidence to happily set aside our positions in favour of building trust-based relationships that facilitate more effective, collaborative, and creative organisations. Only then do we experience the positive mental health and wellbeing we are looking for.

Viktor Frankl, the psychoanalyst incarcerated in Auschwitz, famously said, 'Between stimulus and response there is a space. In that space is our power to choose our response. In our response lies our growth and our freedom.' These principles are about that space – the pause just after what happens for me and what happens for you, where both of us can choose to show up in the space between to let it influence our thinking. They might feel counter-intuitive – after all, our biological inclination is to respond to threat or risk by entering a state of survival – but when we let them live in our relationships in an embodied, felt way, they allow a transformational change in the way we relate to one another.

When I sat in the salon all those years ago and witnessed the conversation between the young woman and the hairdresser, I knew that the only way to redeem that situation was to pause. Stop. What is happening for you? By asking permission to share this question, I stepped into the space between those two people and asked them to join me – not to see who was 'right' and who was 'wrong', but to find out about their experiences. What is happening for you? What is happening for the other? And what is happening between you? The minute the woman said 'I feel ugly,' the salon owner was able to relate to her. They both stepped away from blame and defence and into a space of vulnerability, self-awareness, and reflection where something more powerful could happen.

This is the dance we are invited to take part in every minute of our lives. It is the flow of traffic, the way we navigate each other with presence, curiosity, reflection, candour, and vulnerability. It is the knowledge that, whatever the rupture, there is a way to repair it in order to create greater resilience and relationship.

ONE THING AT A TIME

There is a wonderful word in Japanese – *kaizen*. It is the idea that positive change can happen gradually and slowly if we continue to improve in a methodical way. At work, *kaizen* represents the small, incremental changes that can have a huge impact on the future of an organisation – improvements that can come from any employee at any time. Everyone has a stake in the organisation's success, and everyone can take a small step towards achieving it.

I believe we can apply *kaizen* to building relational capacity. If you pay attention to just one element in the following pages – be it a principle, an individual practice, or a process you can adopt to navigate conversations – you will begin to experience greater regulation and integration. You'll also begin to have different *experiences* in your interactions with your colleagues, your employees, your friends, and your family. It is these positive felt experiences that make powerful change possible.

Building relational capacity takes time, both individually and collectively, so I encourage you to give yourself permission to bed down just one thing at a time – feeling it so that it is embodied, so that it becomes part of your way of being, rather than 'learning' it as a skill or a tool you can use. That might mean reading the remaining chapters in this book in one go and then picking one to focus on, or it might mean dipping in and out as you learn to embody and apply the principles in everyday interactions. Either way, as you grow and embed these ideas in your everyday life and workplace, you will see the interconnectedness of the principles and how they have the power to prevent divides, politics, anxiety, stress, burnout, and depression in the organisation and among the individuals who work there.

Let's begin with presence, as it defines how we show up in the space between.

CHAPTER 4

PRESENCE

"Presence is a willingness to connect beyond surface-level exchanges."

THE CONVERSATION THAT DIDN'T HAPPEN

We all know what it's like to be on the receiving end of someone's lack of presence in a conversation. If we are honest, we also know what it is like to fail to be present ourselves. External distractions, such as unfinished tasks, a never-ending to-do list, or unread emails, as well as internal feelings of anxiety, stress, or overwhelm can make us distant, inattentive, and even ambivalent.

In this sense, being 'present' isn't just about physical proximity. It isn't even about whether we are paying attention to what the other is saying. We can *appear* to be listening – and in some sense we are – but still not be able to truly hear.

So what is presence? The best way to describe it is as an **availability** and an **attunement**: a deep awareness of what is happening for us, for the person we are in connection with, and in the space between us that allows us to fully take part in the conversation.

Here's an example. You head over to your colleague and say 'Do you have a minute?'

They say 'Sure', so you start to tell them your concerns about the project you are working on. But as you talk, you notice they look back at their laptop every time an email notification pops up. You continue, ignoring the distraction, but deep down forming the opinion they are not truly interested in what you have to say. Concluding that your issue is unimportant to them, you start to talk less, minimising the issue you wanted to raise and failing to say what's truly on your mind. You leave their desk feeling ignored and unimportant, confirming an internalised belief that you just don't matter.

Imagine now that the conversation took a different and equally frustrating turn. When you go over to your colleague they shut their laptop and turn to face you. After you talk for a while, they start to seem impatient. They interrupt you, offering solutions before you've finished describing your problem. Experiencing both irritation and a sense of being unheard, you try to put your point across in a different way. You repeat yourself and raise your voice. You end up talking over each other, each failing to hear what the other has to say. You leave feeling angry, unimportant, and deflated.

In both these exchanges, your colleague was physically present. In the second example, they were even mentally present, making an effort to show up and engage with the content of the conversation. Yet in both cases they were not truly attuned to you or the conversation. In the first, this was due to distraction – perhaps an important email exchange or an unfinished task they were experiencing stress about. In the second, it was due to them wanting to find a solution without fully hearing what you had to say.

Presence is about more than taking part. It involves being attuned – to what is being said and to what is happening for us, for the other, and in the space between. The lack of it is felt both within us and in the relational space itself.

In Ed Tronick's Still Face Experiment, which I described in chapter 3, the baby's response to its mother withdrawing her presence was to attempt to regain it. It is the same for us. When we feel someone lacks presence, we try to reconnect with them in any way we can. If we have developed an anxious attachment style, that might mean we repeat ourselves in the hope the person will hear and validate us, or apologise for taking up their time in the hope they won't dismiss us. If we are avoidantly attached, we might simply stop talking and go silent, withdrawing our own presence to match the unavailability of the other person and thus prevent the pain we experience from being seen and heard. Either way, what was happening for us and what was happening for the other hasn't been fully explored, our needs haven't been met, and neither of us has truly heard what the other had to say. You could say that the conversation never happened at all.

If presence is difficult to cultivate in person, imagine how much more challenging it is to create online. In virtual meetings, because we struggle to get a physical impression of their internal state, we must work even harder to read the other's biological cues, increasing our cognitive loads. The social nervous system – that part of us that craves connection – will then fail to receive the validation it needs in order to know the space is safe. Add to this our tendency to multitask, the existence of our underlying survival mode due to our need to mitigate risk, and the differences between generations in organisations today, and true presence has become harder to maintain and vanishingly rare.

This lack of relational 'satiation' has a price. It leads to physical and emotional experiences of isolation, anxiety, depression, and disconnection. It also reinforces our habit of retreating into past narratives rather than engaging with the here and now. In the conversation above, how easy would it be for my colleague to think I am needy, complaining, and a troublemaker? And how easy for me to think they are uninterested, self-absorbed, and arrogant? A conversation where one or both of you are not fully there is far worse than a waste of time. It allows narratives to be written, felt experiences to be embedded, and biases to be constructed that will affect the relationship between the two of you and all future conversations as well. In this way, 'presence' is more literal than we think: when we lack it, we are operating in the 'there and then', not the here and now.

As relational beings, we cry out for presence – our own and that of others. But to get it, we need to prioritise and cultivate our ability to be available, creating conditions that allow us to both self-regulate and co-regulate with the other person. It is only then that conversations can actually start to happen.

Let's go back to the office scenario above and find out what would have happened if you had both been fully present. When you head over to your colleague and say 'Do you have a minute?' they say something different.

'Sure, I just need to finish this email. I need five minutes to do that then I'm all yours.' And they finish writing the email, send it, shut their laptop, and look you straight in the eye. 'Right. What would you like to talk about?'

This simple but profound action – sharing with honesty what you need to do before you can be fully present – allows the other person to know they are valuable. By being available for them, you show them they can feel safe in the space between you. This supports their system to come out of whatever survival state it might be in and start being present themselves. In other words, you have co-regulated the interaction *together*.

Being present is both an individual and a relational activity. When we do it together, we invite the other person to co-create the relational space with us. There is a certain honesty and directness about this, which, if done in service of an effective conversation that allows us to get what we need, is never threatening or judgemental. It is asking someone 'Do you want to read that message before we carry on talking?' or 'I can hear there is a lot on your mind. What is the one thing you'd like me to know?' It is these simple, humble reminders – expressed in the language that feels natural to you – that facilitate presence not just for ourselves, but for the other, too.

Of course, co-regulation can occur only when we are accountable for our responses. This is why true presence is about more than giving your full attention without distractions. It is about being actively available and attuned to what is happening for you so you can take steps to reflect, regulate, and reconnect. It is focusing on your breath when you feel overwhelmed, hearing someone's perspective without planning your response, setting aside your own narrative to avoid filtering their words. It is responding to the subtle cues they give you; for example, noticing when someone's tone of voice shifts and gently asking 'What's happening for you?' It is responding rather than reacting – staying calm and thoughtful in a situation of stress rather than becoming defensive or dismissive.

PRESENCE IS CONTAGIOUS

Self-regulation starts with being aware of what is happening for us in the moment. This is about noticing not just our emotions, but what is happening in our bodies. When we notice this, we can start to make meaning of it. Recognising that the nervous system is activated in a certain way and the physiological sensations that go with that is the first step to truly showing up in a conversation. It is saying to yourself, *My stomach is churning before this conversation. I think that's because I have an ongoing narrative that it will go badly based on past experience.*

In this way, presence is about a connection. You might feel that you are fully present but be harbouring something that is preventing you from showing up fully. Self-regulation allows us to come out of survival mode, think about our thinking, and increase our relational capacity so we can be with the person we are meeting. When we do, we start to navigate the differences between us without becoming positional, defensive, blaming, or withdrawn.

The HeartMath Institute is a scientific research centre that has been exploring the heart–brain connection for thirty years. This connection is based on the fact our heart rates are always changing, creating a pattern called heart rate variability. When we are in survival mode – a state of high stress – this heart-rhythm pattern is erratic and disordered. This inhibits the brain's ability to complete higher cognitive functions like thinking clearly, remembering, learning, reasoning, and making decisions. Simply put, our heart rates affect our ability to think.

What is less known is that the heart's rhythm also affects the brain's emotional processes. The felt experience of stress (for example, when we are in survival mode) not only affects our heart rhythm but feeds back to the brain itself. In this way, it reinforces itself in a loop of stress, emotion, and dysregulation.

On the other hand, when the heart's rhythm is more stable – for example, in times of calm – we have better cognitive function and a more regulated nervous system response. And as we know from Polyvagal Theory, this affects the nervous system of the other person by giving biological cues that the space between us is safe and unthreatening. So our own regulated nervous systems actually regulate the nervous system of the other, creating a sort of heart-rhythm coherence that helps us to co-regulate. In this way, presence isn't just co-created. It's contagious.

AVOIDING PRESENCE

Presence is one of the most meaningful gifts we can offer. When we are truly present, we enable ourselves and others to feel seen, valued, and connected, and we create a relational space where we can experience being known and appreciated ourselves.

So why do we avoid presence? As comforting as the idea of being fully available seems, it can also provoke fear. This is because escape often feels safer than confronting the unknowns that come with genuine presence. Being fully in the here and now rather than the there and then gives us challenges we'd sometimes rather not face. It forces us to confront the narratives we hold about ourselves (*I'm a nuisance*), the other (*she's always difficult*), and the space between us (*these conversations never go well*). In survival mode, we rely even more on these 'old photographs' – the frozen snapshots of who we believe others are and what they're capable of – to tell us the story we know. This narrative keeps us safe, reinforcing assumptions and avoiding the vulnerability of making ourselves fully present. By continually referencing these photographs, we mitigate risk by confirming our beliefs about people: the manager who is always critical, the meeting where I am never heard. By holding tight to these images, we avoid the discomfort of confronting the unknown, of risking a different interaction, and of forming a new perception.

This is why making meaning from our responses is so important. Noticing them and stepping up into our thinking in order to make sense of them is how a self-regulated person becomes a grounded and stable anchor in the relational space.

WHOLE BODY LEARNING

So how is this done? One of the scariest things for a human being is to be swimming in an ocean of emotions, so the first step to self-regulation is to learn how to effectively pay attention to what is happening for us. This means first being able to name what is happening for you and understanding how this experience influences you, the other, and the relational health of your team and organisation.

Our thoughts are not separate from our bodies. In fact, the way we relate to the world and create meaning involves our entire neural network and emotions – even if we're not aware of it.

What happens for you when I ask, 'What is 14 + 23 - 7 × 41?' Take a moment now to notice your internal response – because although this is a mathematical task, which, in theory, requires no emotion, you will still have an emotional response. You will experience fear, panic, excitement, shame, embarrassment, frustration, or disappointment – or any combination of the above – depending on your past experience of solving mathematical problems.

Whole body learning is what happens when we pay attention to that experience. It allows us to notice what is happening for us, to voice it, and to start to make meaning from it. It goes beyond thoughts and instead asks, *What happens in my body when I hear that?* This isn't about finding solutions, but about simply reflecting on what occurs for us, noticing the emotion, validating it, and allowing ourselves to experience it. Only then can we move *out* of that emotion and take our attention further up, away from what we are experiencing to our more cerebral thinking about that emotion.

I call this 'taking the elevator'. If you imagine your sensations, emotions, and thoughts as a triangle on its base, your sensations and emotions would be at the bottom two points. Your thoughts – your mental processing of those emotions that happens in the prefrontal cortex – are at the top. Moving from emotion to thinking about that emotion requires us to take the elevator up to that higher level – to listen to our whole body in order to regulate our physical sensations and our emotions.

Like all the practices in this book, whole body learning can be done alone or with another person. I did it when I witnessed that heated conversation at the hairdresser's. I stopped them and simply asked, 'What's happening for you as you hear that?' This allowed both Carl and his client to pause, reflect, and think about their experiences.

This is why presence is not just an individual endeavour. It is a shared practice requiring intentionality. This almost always begins with noticing. For example, in a meeting where too many people are talking or one person is 'dumping' too much information, we would notice and ask the question 'There's a lot being said here. Shall we all take a moment just to breathe, take a walk around and stretch our legs so we can really hear each other?'

Or, in a meeting where people are distracted by technology, the noticing would be the suggestion 'I notice a number of us have been distracted by our phones. I realise there is a lot going on and wonder if we need to take a moment to answer messages and emails so we can come back to being here in this meeting?' Sometimes it is the simple acknowledgement of emotions through validation: 'It makes sense to me you are frustrated given you only had two hours to pull together a presentation that usually takes six.'

You'll see that in all these scenarios, presence is created by addressing what we instinctively try to avoid – the elephant in the room, the real conversation that invites us all into presence so we can discuss what we are here to do. This action might seem like it would cause a delay, but the moments taken to monitor presence and correct the imbalance are never wasted. The results are transformational.

As we go through this book, you will also see that cultivating presence requires us to embody and apply the other principles: reflection, curiosity, respectful candour, vulnerability, navigating difference, being in service of a shared goal, and having a mindset of abundance. In this way, the eight principles work together to pay attention to the *process* of our conversations rather than just the content. You will learn to apply the practices that support this – at first at a cognitive level, but over time in a way that is felt and embodied. These can be used individually and as a team, and in many cases, they take moments. The results are teams, conversations, and cultures that are psychologically safe, empathic, productive, and respectful.

BREATHWORK

Whole body learning will make us aware of our physiological responses to a particular stimulus, and once we are aware of them, there is a lot we can do to regulate. The key to this is breath. It's easy to think of breath as a 'natural thing we do' that needs no attention. Yet, while breathing is automatic (we will stay alive whether we remember to do it or not), it has a powerful effect on our nervous system responses. This is why it has been studied in every culture of the world.

Breath brings oxygen into the body and removes CO2. This affects all our organs, but particularly our brain cells, which require a lot of oxygen. So breathing not only affects how we function physically; it also affects our ability to think. This is because breathing correctly helps to move us out of our sensations – the response that happens in our bodies – and take the elevator up to the brain, where we can process those sensations with rational thought. This enables us to ask more linear, focused, and pragmatic questions, such as *Am I able to be present for this conversation? What is preventing me from doing so? What can I do to increase my presence, or do I need to postpone this interaction until I am more available?*

Focusing on and regulating breath can change our ability to self-regulate – and therefore increase our presence – in moments. We can also use breath to co-regulate – to invite others to make meaning of their own experiences and the space between us in the room. This allows us all to take the elevator up – to increase our presence and to be more available for the conversations that need to happen.

So how do we do this? By slowing down the breath, paying attention to how it enters and leaves the body, and choosing from where we breathe into and out. With practice, you will find which breathing exercises work best for you, but below are two you can try to give yourself permission to notice any physical, emotional, or cognitive impact your breath has on your ability to be in the here and now.

The physiological sigh (cyclic sighing)

1. Take one very long, deep inhalation through your nose.
2. When you think you have completely inflated your lungs, take a second, quick inhalation through your mouth and hold it for a second.
3. Fully exhale through your mouth until your lungs are completely empty.

You will find the second inhalation in this exercise difficult – it requires additional physical vigour to add air to your already full lungs. One single physiological sigh when you are preparing for a meeting you are likely to find challenging is the fastest way to reduce stress and reintroduce calm to the autonomic nervous system. You can also do this exercise after a meeting or conversation or, if your colleagues are available and willing, together as a team during a meeting where presence has waned.

Box breathing

1. While sitting down, breathe normally in and out through your nose for ten seconds.
2. Then inhale through your nose as much as you can.
3. Using a timer, measure how long it takes to deliberately control the exhalation until your lungs are empty. This is your CO2 discard rate.
4. Give yourself a score based on how long it took you to expel all your air: three if it took you twenty seconds or less, five to six if it took you between twenty-five and forty-five seconds, and eight to ten if it took you over forty-six seconds.
5. Now do two minutes of box breathing (inhale, hold, exhale, hold) using the number you got in the exercise; e.g., six-second inhalation, six-second hold, six-second exhalation, six-second hold.

This exercise increases your neural mechanical control of the diaphragm by deliberately focusing on and taking control of the way you expel CO2. This leads to changes in the resting pattern of your breathing, helping you stay calm under pressure, reducing stress, aiding sleep, and reducing the chances of hyperventilation when faced with a challenging situation.

Interestingly, when Dr David Spiegel's team at Stanford University studied these breathing methods and compared them to meditation, they found that deliberate breathwork practices done for five minutes a day over the course of a month led to greater reductions in stress than a five-minute meditation.[7]

It is worth noting here that self-regulation through breathwork and whole body learning isn't about trying to control our emotions or sensations. There is nothing more exhausting than being with someone who is trying to keep a lid on how they feel. Instead, it is about riding emotions like a wave, experiencing them with curiosity and then moving up into our thinking so that we can be empathic, connected, and relational.

BUILDING PRESENCE IN ORGANISATIONS

Individual practices like the ones above play a crucial role in helping us embed presence in our day-to-day lives. But organisations can also prioritise and support presence by facilitating these practices in their processes and culture.

I have found that in many organisations there is a disconnect between the facilities they offer and the true level of their relational capacity. They might talk about empowerment and offer mindfulness courses, wellbeing seminars, workshops, and one-to-one therapy, but are peopled with individuals who micromanage, create unhealthy competition, and demand agility and productivity over true relationality and connection.

Ironically, when employees are allowed and encouraged to be truly present, they are more productive, more collaborative, more connected, more resilient, more motivated, make fewer mistakes, and solve problems more easily.

As a leader – even if that means you are simply running a meeting – you are responsible for checking on your team's presence. You can do this by asking if anyone came straight from another meeting or presentation. Are people pulled in multiple directions? Employees cannot be in the here and now if they are not given time to notice their presence before it is asked of them.

Leaders who embody relational presence create safe relational spaces. By being available for co-regulation, they set the tone for the entire team or organisation, promoting resilience and collaboration instead of risk mitigation and fear. But real change demands that we risk being present – that we open ourselves to the possibility of a shared reality rather than clinging to our internalised narratives. This means creating a new, shared narrative, letting go of old stories, and being available in the here and now for a new way. Only then do we have the potential to see others – and ourselves – with fresh eyes, allowing new possibilities for connection, understanding, and transformation to emerge.

PRACTICES TO SUPPORT PRESENCE

In order to understand and effectively tune into what is happening in the relational space, we need to start with ourselves. We need to understand how we function, learn about our beliefs and what influences us, as well as pay attention to the way we think, our emotions, and what we are sensing in our bodies.

Here are some ways you can increase your presence in day-to-day life:

1. Before any conversation or meeting, take two minutes to breathe and connect with what you are going to be doing. This helps you arrive in the meeting grounded and available to hear and 'resets' your nervous system to move you out of a state of survival and into one of availability.
2. Listen to the whole of your body. What is happening for you right now? What is your heartbeat like? Do you feel any tension in your jaw, stomach, or neck? What is your breathing like? Where is it coming from? Is it fast or slow?
3. Now take the elevator up. Why might you be sensing these experiences? Can you name these sensations and emotions?
4. Be honest with yourself and the other person. Sometimes we simply cannot be present and we must take responsibility for our quality of presence and for the impact that lack of presence will have on the other: 'I really would like to hear your thinking about that project. I'm aware that I'd probably struggle to give you my full attention right now. Could we regroup at 4 p.m.?'
5. Give clear signals that show you are present. Put your phone away, shut your laptop, face the other person, perhaps even move from behind a desk to sit opposite them so there is nothing between you. These biological cues help to co-regulate with the other person by showing them the space is safe.

6. If you notice your quality of presence dipping or you become distracted, be honest: 'Apologies, I notice I became distracted there. Would you mind if I just write down what was in my head so I can come back and hear you properly?' This prevents the other person from creating their own narrative when they notice your distraction (which they will) and changing the way they themselves show up in the space between you.

Breathwork, noticing, communicating your availability and attunement, and taking the elevator up from sensations and emotions will all help to facilitate presence in your organisation and your teams. Once we learn to apply these practices, we will, over time, embody them as a felt experience. Yet there is more work to be done. While breathwork can help us regulate our responses enough to get through a meeting, a conversation, an interaction, or a discussion, to have true presence we must be willing to risk something more. We must delve further – into how we function and make meaning of the world around us – so we can truly change how we relate and respond to other people. This is what brings transformational change to our teams, our relationships, and our organisations, and for this, our presence is not enough.

In becoming present we must be willing to pause there and reflect.

START WITH THIS

With any kind of change, trying to do too much at once can feel overwhelming. So start by reflecting on your presence.

If you were to give your presence a percentage, what would that be?

Is it 80%, 50%? Maybe it is only 10% or 20%. If it is anything below 100% then ask, *What do I need to do to increase my quality of presence by 5%?*

This could be putting away your phone, turning off notifications, using a timer, doing a breathing exercise, stretching, taking five minutes outside, walking around the block, or simply washing your hands.

When you have done one of these simple things, ask yourself again, *What's the percentage of my presence right now?*

CHAPTER 5

REFLECTION – EXAMINING OUR THOUGHTS, EMOTIONS, AND ACTIONS

"Ask yourself:
What's the one thing that
needs to happen before
anything else can happen?"

COUNTING TO TEN

Increasing presence in our teams and organisations allows us to go beyond the *content* of the conversation and notice what is *happening* in it – for us, for the other person, and in the space between. When we do, we open a world where our interactions occur not just on a surface level, but in a way that increases our capacity to relate to each other in the here and now. This is vital for creating high-functioning teams and organisations: conversations become less charged, people are less reactive, and interactions are less oppositional, all because we're available and attuned to what's really going on.

Being present opens a world of opportunity – to go beyond what is being said and find out more about ourselves, the other, and the way we relate to each other. This takes us to a deeper level of conversation where we don't just react, but make sense of how we function.

When you were a child, you probably displayed your emotions quite openly. As you got older and understood what was appropriate in certain situations, you learnt to suppress those emotions as needed. Now, as an adult in the workplace, you no doubt have conversations where you experience all sorts of emotions – irritation, defensiveness, anxiety, fear – but you're able to override what's happening in your body and control how you react. In fact, you might have become so used to doing this, the emotion barely gets heard at all. You've become an expert in wearing the mask. You bite your lip, turn the other cheek, count to ten.

In chapter 3, I quoted neurologist, psychiatrist, and Holocaust survivor Viktor Frankl. 'Between stimulus and response', he said, 'there is a space. In that space is our power to choose our response.' What Frankl is talking about here is that moment when we feel like we need to count to ten. We might not even notice it, because we've become so used to brushing it away. Yet Frankl was right: in the split second between what someone says to us and the reaction we give in return, we have an opportunity to pause.

Developing the presence we talked about in the last chapter helps us to do that. By pausing in that space, we give ourselves time to notice our emotions – not necessarily how we *feel*, but what is happening for us on an autonomic, or physiological, level. If we can breathe and self-regulate that response, we can take ourselves out of survival mode and learn to respond rather than react.

Yet truly relating with each other requires more. Rather than simply pausing in the gap between stimulus and response in order to somehow 'control' our reactions, we must learn to make sense of what has happened. This allows us to discover meaning about ourselves and the world so we not only respond more relationally in the here and now but have a more regulated and relational response in the future. Transformation of our relationships happens only when we go this step further, stepping back to think about our thinking rather than learning to count to ten. This is reflection, and it's where we begin to bridge the gap between what happens *to* us and what happens *for* us.

In the last chapter, I asked what happened for you when you were asked to solve a mathematical problem. By noticing your response – perhaps fear, panic, shame, or excitement – you immediately increased your ability to be present in the here and now. Now think about that response again. If you experienced panic or fear, where might that have come from? What meaning could you make from it? This is the essence of reflection: thinking about your thinking. It's the difference between noticing what happens for you and understanding the meaning of that response.

Reflecting in this way is essential for our personal growth, emotional wellbeing, and social functioning because evaluating our experiences in the past, the present, and the future activates three important parts of the brain: the posterior cingulate cortex, the anterior cingulate cortex, and the medial prefrontal cortex. These are responsible for reformulating our understanding of ourselves in relation to others and in a socially contextualised way.

Without reflecting on what happens – for us, the other, and in the space between – we will struggle to build teams that relate to each other effectively and with compassion, because the mirror neurons required for empathy will not be activated. In fact, we will only ever be able to regulate our responses on a surface level, failing to understand *why* we respond and how it might affect the people around us. We will then struggle to create a culture of openness, belonging, and trust, because we haven't made meaning of the way we work.

To do this, we need to take the risk of stepping into that gap. Let me show you what that looks like – and what it doesn't.

THE POST-MORTEM ANALYSIS

In teams, 'reflection' often takes the form of analysis: 'How did we do? What went wrong? What could we do differently next time?' This often happens at a post-mortem meeting. You might be familiar with this scenario.

Imagine a team has completed a project that didn't meet client expectations. It was over budget, delivered late, and riddled with errors – and everyone has their own story about why. The project manager sends an email invitation to everyone involved, with the subject heading 'Post-mortem analysis'.

At the start of the meeting, the project manager begins by saying, 'Personally, I'd like to share how frustrated and discouraged I am with the outcome of this project. We missed every deadline, every milestone, and came in 15% over budget. We also have an unhappy client – just this morning I had to take a phone call explaining how utterly disappointed they are with the result. So, I want to know from each of you what went wrong and how we can prevent this from happening again. Who'd like to start?'

The room is silent. People look down at their notebooks, focusing on anything to avoid eye contact with the project manager. Eventually, someone is brave enough to speak: 'Well, I said from the beginning that I was anxious about the timeline. If I'd been listened to we could have revised it to something more realistic.'

Someone else speaks up. 'We did listen, but the tech team never made it a priority. We could have had all the time in the world, but without their commitment we were always going to fail.'

A member of the tech team says 'That's unfair. We were working overtime to get on top of our other projects already. Were we just supposed to drop one of those?'

The manager cuts in with 'If your workload was a problem, that should have been communicated straight away. Part of the role is to prioritise projects.'

The team member is about to respond but holds back. Meanwhile, someone else jumps in. 'I think it's an issue of project management. If someone had checked in on how we were doing then we would have known about the timeline issues earlier.'

The original team member is exasperated. 'I did – I said from the outset the timeline was unrealistic. Why doesn't anyone ever listen?'

And on it goes.

If this scenario is familiar, it's because it's all too common. Everyone adopts their positions, no one is willing to concede, emotions run high... and the more analysis there is, the more resentful everyone in the team feels.

The consequences of this kind of 'reflection' go far beyond the meeting at hand. By blaming, shaming, adopting positions, and refusing to consider what's happening for anyone else, the team not only fails to reach a solution but creates ruptures, biases, and beliefs that extend far into the next project.

This isn't from a lack of trying. I'd be willing to bet everyone in that meeting thought long and hard about what had gone wrong on the project. They probably analysed it for days. Yet by ruminating on whose fault it was, rather than reflecting on the thoughts, sensations, and emotions behind it, no one was able to make meaning of anything that had happened. While they had all *experienced* their responses, they hadn't taken time to understand what those responses might mean.

Analysis is not reflection. Neither is rumination, evaluation, blame, self-control, or keeping a lid on what's on our minds. When we focus on what happened as an *event* rather than what happened for us *internally*, we can only ever remain trapped by our emotional experiences. This renders us unable to make meaning of the physical and emotional sensations we have or come to any sort of helpful conclusion to the problem at hand.

The conflict that ensues increases our anxiety around our emotions, pushing us into the trap of hyper-analysing our positions rather than paying attention to why we've processed things as we have. The result is that we confirm our own narratives, strengthen our biases around other people, and act these out in self-defence the next time a similar situation occurs. We'll then struggle to improve the way we relate to other people, because we haven't given the rupture the chance to repair.

I wonder what would have happened in this meeting if it had been different from the start. What if, instead of sending an impersonal meeting invitation that immediately put the team into survival mode, the project manager had emailed 'I thought it would be good to take some time to reflect on the recent project. Is that something you'd be up for? Please could you let me know by the end of tomorrow.'

By asking people to confirm their presence first, wouldn't she have given the team more of an opportunity to pause? And wouldn't they then have assessed their availability to have the conversation, immediately being able to regulate their nervous system responses?

I think that by knowing everyone was available to have the meeting in the first place, the manager would then have been more able to invite them to reflect. The conversation could then have gone a little more like this: 'As you all know, this project didn't deliver what we said we would. If it's OK, I'd like to hear what we individually and collectively found challenging. Who'd be willing to start?'

By focusing on what happened for the team members themselves rather than what happened to make the project fail, the manager would have allowed them to notice their physical and emotional experiences. As a result, I think the first team member's response would have looked a lot more like this: 'For me it was the timeline. It was just too tight, and right from the start I was anxious about it. I did try to raise it, but no one was prepared to listen.'

The manager could then have replied 'You're right, you did. OK, so I'm getting that you were anxious about the timeline. Can you tell me what about that felt challenging? Was it that we were afraid to lose the client and therefore set an unrealistic timeline, or was it that we didn't have enough resources to complete the task? Or was it something else?'

This would have allowed the team member to reflect not on what others did wrong, but on their experience of the project feeling out of hand. 'Well, we definitely didn't have the resources. I felt like I was always behind. It got to the stage where it was consuming my life.'

The manager could then have responded 'It's understandable that it was consuming your life, it was a big project. OK, so, beyond more resources, what did you need from us as a team?'

'I needed someone from tech to ask if there was anything they could do – even if there wasn't.'

'And how would that have helped?'

'It would have showed me someone cared. I wouldn't have felt so alone.'

Reflection takes us away from blame and shame and down to the unmet need. This is the difference between analysis – trying to work out what's happened from a cognitive perspective – and reflection – taking into account thoughts, emotions, and sensations as a process of whole body learning. In this case, it revealed the team member's need to not feel alone in their overwhelm and to know that what they were doing mattered. By addressing this before future projects, the next one is already set up for more success.

It's only when we tackle analysis like this – by reflecting on our human, emotional needs – that we allow for the process of repair. By co-creating a shared understanding, we go beyond 'what went wrong' and show we're willing to hear, understand, and learn from one another without adopting an adversarial stance. This builds psychological safety and reinforces the idea that mistakes and tensions are opportunities for growth.

REFLECTION IN THE HERE AND NOW

What I hope the example above shows is that reflection is a choice. It's an intentional pause that enables us to make meaning of our responses. This helps us look at our experiences in a way that determines not only what happened, but what happened for *us*.

Although reflection, by its nature, often happens after an event, we can also do this in the here and now. This, as Frankl says, is the pause at the point of interaction, the split-second gap between stimulus and response where we choose how we're going to react. By reflecting, we notice what is happening for us on a level beyond words: the physical manifestation of our anxiety, defensiveness, panic, fear, anger, resentment, or frustration.

The power of this is immeasurable because when we notice and name our sensations, we immediately understand the conversation as a *process* rather than just on the level of what is being said.

I was once working with a senior executive when he noticed this process in play. One day he asked me, 'Kerry-Lyn, I've noticed you often say things like "What happens for you when I say that?" or "Can you tell me more?" Why do you do that?'

Like any good politician, I answered with a question: 'What's it like for you when I do that?'

He paused. Then he said, 'It makes me reflect on what's going on underneath, not just on what's been said. Then I feel more in control because I'm *noticing* how I feel rather than just letting that emotion affect others. I really want to learn how to do this with my team.'

Inviting someone to reflect makes them pause in the here and now. It invites them to notice and name what's happening for them in order to understand more about themselves and their response. In doing so, their nervous system is calmed, they feel heard and understood, and they don't need to enter survival mode, because I'm relating with them in the space between. Then it doesn't matter what the conversation is about – the process itself is a safe place to be.

SLOWING DOWN

'This all sounds well and good,' you might say, 'but the reality is most conversations happen in a matter of seconds. How do we take time to reflect in a world that moves at a hundred miles per hour?'

We have a saying in psychotherapy: 'It takes fifteen seconds to process a thought'. This isn't necessarily literal – it just means our brains take a while to catch up. In this sense, we are constantly living slightly in the past. This is a survival mechanism, protecting us from the overwhelm of a constantly changing environment. Evidence suggests we do this with our eyes, too, 'merging' visual input over a period of seconds in order to create a more stable view of the world.[8] Emotions take even longer to process than thoughts because they engage more complex and prolonged neural pathways. This is why therapists often make room for long periods of silence, especially when exploring challenging issues.

It's also why meetings like the one above – conducted at speed and without time for participants to truly reflect – so often end in dysregulation and dissent. By interacting at speed, we don't allow our brains to catch up enough to make meaning of what's going on.

This can also happen when online interactions haven't been preceded by building in-person relationships. Without a bedrock of reflection and understanding, written communication – for example, by email or on platforms like Slack – can cause more people to enter a survival state and exacerbate an anxious attachment style. This is because it's easier to depersonalise and objectify another person when you can't hear their tone of voice, can't see their face, and can't connect with their heart coherence. We only have to remember the personal impact of Google laying off hundreds of its workforce by email to see this is true.

So what's the solution? One thing all the relational principles in this book have in common is that they force us to slow down. By reflecting, we add an extra step in the process of communication – an invitation to stop and notice what is happening for us before we respond. We can see how well this works in the revised version of the post-mortem meeting above: by asking the team to confirm their presence and willingness to reflect, the manager paved the way for a more regulated and productive meeting, even at the start.

Allowing time to pay attention to what's happening for us, the other, and in the space between gives us the opportunity to reflect on our responses *before* they disrupt the way we relate to each other. By noticing and naming what's happening – whether that's an emotion, a survival state, a bias, an assumption, or an attachment style – we're able to self-regulate and *co-regulate* with others in service of the conversation we need to have.

REFLECTION AS A PATH TO RECONNECTION

Slowing down also allows us to pay attention to the other's experience. In most conversations, this is where we get stuck. We're so contained by our own agendas that we pay attention only to the expression of the other person's emotion and not the emotion itself. A manifestation of aggression, sulking, or defensiveness; a tendency to talk over people; repetition; withdrawal; or any combination of the above is less important than what's happening to cause that response. By paying attention to the behaviour rather than why it might occur, it's all too easy to make up our own narratives. This is then based not on the other person's real experience, but on our biases and beliefs about what their behaviour means.

When we come to the conversation with reflection, however, it's a different story. Having taken meaning from and self-regulated our responses, we're in a better position to notice and understand what's happening for the other person – especially if we take the time to ask. In this sense, reflection, just like presence, is something we do together as well as alone.

When the project manager in the meeting above asked the team to share what they found challenging, she allowed them to take the elevator up from their emotions and think about their experiences on a more cognitive level. Now they could take time to reflect on what had happened for them – not just in the project, but at that moment in the room. Once they did this, they opened the opportunity for reconnection in a space without blame, identifying the need that was unmet and understanding what would have met that need.

Reflecting, regulating, and reconnecting like this is infinitely more valuable than dissecting what went wrong, because rather than focusing on actions it improves the relationships within the team. By removing the distraction of blame and focusing on repairing whatever rupture has taken place, we create more psychological safety, greater collaboration, and increased productivity – not just in that team, but in the organisation as a whole.

BUILDING REFLECTION IN ORGANISATIONS

Making space for reflection might feel like time you cannot afford to give. After all, most teams and organisations feel the need to run at speed. Without pausing to slow the stimulus–response process, however, you will find the same mistakes being made. This is because the same narratives will rerun, the same issues will prevail, and the same misunderstandings and disagreements will occur. Worse than this, the exact same relationship divides will continue to prevent your teams from collaborating with the productivity and efficiency you need.

In the moment the project manager allowed her team to reflect, she provided the opportunity to discover the emotional needs behind their positions. By pausing, she created the conditions for the right conversation to occur and allowed the team to move forward to a solution based on learning, rather than blame and shame. As a bonus, they all had a positive felt experience of what it's like to be heard.

Reflecting as a team allows us to communicate what we need. It also shows others what we want them to understand – about our stress responses, our thought processes, our attachment styles, and our worlds. This helps us work together to understand how we tend to respond, why we respond the way we do, and how those responses contribute to the relational space. We then make more meaning of our attachment styles and understand how they might clash with those of others, learning to regulate and reconnect to avoid similar clashes in future. In this way, reflection isn't a waste of time but an investment – ensuring from now on you have the one conversation you need to have, instead of a series of meetings that do more harm than good.

Reflection in organisations – whether it's in teams, meetings, or external relationships – always starts with a question. For me, the first question is the most important: 'What's the one thing that needs to happen here before anything else can happen?'

I ask myself this constantly during therapy sessions, meetings, presentations, and group work in organisations because it helps me focus on what's happening in the here and now. The answer is often pragmatic: it might be to give people time to read the meeting notes, to take a few deep breaths to increase their presence after a previous meeting, or to get up and walk around if they've been sitting for a long time. It might be to ask everyone to write down what they would like to get from the meeting and share it, or even to ask if the meeting is necessary in the first place.

Once we've established this, the process can continue with other reflective questions, asked either by individuals internally or together as a group. These could include:

- What am I paying attention to right now?
- What is the purpose of my input?
- What is happening for me in my body?
- How can I self-regulate?
- How can I co-regulate with the people in this room?
- What does each of them need from me?
- Do I feel heard and understood?
- Do they?
- Am I understanding what they are saying, or am I thinking about my own agenda?

These questions might seem simple, but they open the door to high-functioning teams. You can ask them in advance or in the here and now, even taking time in meetings to stop and ask 'What's happening for everyone as we talk about this?' Whether together or alone, reflecting on what's happening, what we might learn from it, and how it might affect what happens in the space between us allows us to reach solutions to problems, rather than creating new problems instead. This makes teams more trusting, more self-aware, and more empathic in their relationships with each other.

PRACTICES TO SUPPORT REFLECTION

Creating teams of people who understand their responses and allowing that understanding to influence them takes practice. As ever, that practice starts with us. Here are some ways you can increase your ability to reflect in day-to-day life:

1. Before you respond next time, take a pause to WAIT. This stands for Why Am I Talking? It allows you to reflect more deeply on what is driving you to speak. Do you have a need to be seen? Is your anxious attachment style causing you to feel threatened because you haven't yet contributed? Are you repeating yourself because you want to feel that your role matters? Learning to WAIT helps you understand what you're in service of, what you might need from the other person, and what you believe or assume they might need from you.
2. Before inviting anyone to troubleshoot, analyse, or investigate, first evaluate your and their presence. Are you both in the right frame of mind to do this? Do you have the time? If you need to reschedule the conversation, do so. It's better than causing a rupture you can't repair.
3. Practise slowing down conversations. This gives each of you the opportunity to process and integrate what's being said and what's happening between you. This can be done at the beginning of a conversation or meeting: 'What's the one thing you'd like to get from our time together today?', during it: 'What happens for you as I say that?', or after it: 'What landed for you there, and what did you learn about yourself and the team?'
4. Self-regulate your response. You can do this through breathwork, whole body learning, and taking the elevator up to think about your emotions. You could even

engage a team in breathwork at the start of a meeting. This creates biological cues that the space between you is psychologically safe and allows co-regulation of others' responses as well as your own.

5. Use the right language. Ask 'What happens for you as I say that?' rather than 'How do you feel?' or 'What do you think?' This connects people to their physical responses and enables whole body learning, rather than reactions initiated by emotion.

When we invite people to pay attention to more than their thinking, they begin to notice their *experiences* rather than just their thoughts. This allows them and us to be more present, more reflective, more psychologically safe, and more empathic to those we work with. We then have an opportunity to understand each other more – not just our autonomic responses, but the stories and felt experiences that are behind how we see the world. This takes us outside the limits of right and wrong and to a place that is deeper and wider – to the ultimate position of allowing our thinking to be influenced by the thinking of someone else. To do this, we need to start asking questions in a way we never have before.

START WITH THIS

Reflection requires us to connect with our bodies and minds in the here and now in a way many of us aren't used to. The following exercise gives you the chance to experience what that's like and how our past votes loudly in our present.

Put a piece of chocolate in your mouth. Don't chew or suck it, but rather let it sit there between your tongue and the roof of your mouth. Allow it to melt slowly. Don't be tempted to rush the process, just sit in the knowledge that the chocolate will melt all by itself. Reflect on these questions:

- What sensations do you experience?
- Where do you experience them?
- What emotions do you experience as you notice the sensations?
- What memories come up as you pay attention to the sensations and the emotions?

When the chocolate has completely melted, reflect again with a single question:

- What happened for you as you waited for the sensation to subside?

CHAPTER 6

CURIOSITY – CULTIVATING OPENNESS AND A DESIRE TO LEARN

"Curiosity is the art of letting someone or something else influence our thinking."

WHAT HAPPENS WHEN WE DO NOT KNOW

Pausing to reflect on our experiences – not on how we *feel* when we interact with someone but on what *happens* for us as we do so – allows us to make meaning from our responses. On a personal level this allows us to self-regulate; doing it in teams and organisations transforms the way we work.

In the past, we might have avoided this pause. This is because for many of us reflection feels dangerous – after all, we've been wired to mitigate risk. Reflecting on our experiences might open emotions we'd rather not confront. At work, this is also something we avoid. Like individuals, organisations are trained to look for certainty – not only in their forecasts, budgets, and reviews, but in their thinking, their beliefs, and the cultural relationships within the team.

In fact, certainty is so important to us that when we lack it, we resort to making it up. The narratives we write – about ourselves, others, even things that have happened in the past – quickly become the truth. This has led to what author Robert Greene described as 'the biggest disease the mind faces': as humans, we always prefer knowing to not knowing – even if that means creating the truth ourselves.

Yet teams, like people, are not certain. They are chaotic, unpredictable, unquantifiable, and erratic. We all have our own attachment styles, our biases, our beliefs, and our tendencies to respond in certain ways. We're also all capable of creating our own truths about the people in our teams. How many times have you looked at someone's behaviour and assumed you know what's behind it, allowing a false narrative to take hold before you even know the truth? How many times have you adopted a dogmatic and opinionated approach, arriving at a position in advance and refusing to have it shaped by anything anyone has to say?

The irony about certainty is that the more we desire it, the less we're likely to know. This is because in seeking conviction in what we know, we so often get the story wrong.

THE DANGER OF A SINGLE STORY

In the last chapter, we learnt that reflection is more than 'checking in'. It's pausing to go deeper, to not only notice our responses, but to make meaning from them. To be in true relationship with each other, we need to go further again. We need to let go of our need to be certain and allow ourselves to sit in a place where we do not know.

Imagine you've just come out of a team meeting. You're happy with how it went: the atmosphere in the room was positive, everyone nodded along and contributed to the agenda you'd worked hard to create. You walk away thinking, *Great, everyone's on the same page and knows what they have to do.*

As the week goes on, however, you start to realise that this might not be true. You find yourself having to remind some of the team of their action points or clarify what you asked them to provide. In some cases, people even deliver the wrong work. Then there are the questions, the pushing back on what you thought had been agreed. Despite your impression that everyone was on the same page and knew what to do, you quickly realise that they aren't and they don't.

In time, your frustration shows, and within days you notice discord and alienation within the team. You find yourself going round and round in a cycle of misunderstanding and poor communication, and all the time one question repeats in your mind: *How did I get it so wrong?*

At the end of the meeting, you thought it had gone well. Yet, in being so caught up in what you thought you knew, you missed a vital piece of the puzzle: you didn't ask.

Assumptions like this create discord and disconnection. They perpetuate beliefs, stifle innovation, and hinder collaboration in teams and organisations. In time, they become stories – narratives driven by falsity because we didn't try to find out the truth. Not only does this cause us to become stuck in our thinking, it also prevents us from experiencing the richness and complexity of the relationships that happen when we let our thinking go.

The novelist Chimamanda Ngozi Adichie highlights this in her TED Talk 'The Danger of a Single Story'. She describes how, growing up in Nigeria, she read only British and American children's books. As a result, she had a single story about what English children were like. According to her early writing, they played in the snow, drank ginger beer, and talked endlessly about the weather.

Later, when Adichie went to study in America, she found people had a single story about her life, too. Her roommate was surprised she could speak English, astonished at her impressive education, and taken aback that she knew how to drive a car. Her roommate's single story of Africa was one of poverty, hunger, and corruption – issues that of course exist, but were not Adichie's experience.

Adichie's talk highlights that when we fail to question our assumptions about a person, they become those assumptions. We reduce their experience to a flattened version of the truth – one that is at best incomplete, at worst dangerously incorrect. This is because our need for certainty prevents us from discovering the infinite number of *other* stories that exist for that person. As a result, we deny ourselves the opportunity to find out what's really happening for them, because we think we already know.

In the last chapter, we learnt that reflection is 'thinking about your thinking'. Yet to show up effectively in the way we relate to one another, we must do something more: we must allow someone else's thinking to influence ours. This is curiosity. It asks us to step outside what we *think* we know and open ourselves to what we don't, allowing new narratives about a person as well as new narratives about ourselves.

This is what was lacking in the misunderstanding above. By failing to ask about others' experiences of the meeting, an assumption was made about what we couldn't possibly know. The fallout of this was resentment, confusion, poor communication, and a lack of psychological safety in the team.

For a colleague who is avoidantly attached, the impact of this might be a failure to speak up in the pretence they know what they've got to do. For a more anxiously attached person, it might be taking on the bulk of the work so they'll finally be valued for what they contribute to the team. In both cases, the failure to be curious led to a reliance on a single story rather than the more complex reality of what was happening for each person in that meeting.

Have you ever stopped to think about the single stories you tell yourself? What about the people around you, in your organisation or team? Without curiosity, it's all too easy to arrive at positions in advance and never bother to find out if they're true. When we're curious, however, we open ourselves to a different way. We allow another story, one based on what's actually happening, rather than what we think we already know. By stepping outside our positions and into the space between, we allow someone else's thinking to influence our own. This increases our ability to relate to others, because we let go of certainty once and for all.

In other words, by getting comfortable with what we don't know, we open ourselves to an easier, more collaborative way of working as a team.

ENDLESS POSSIBILITIES

In the meeting described above, the assumption that the team was in agreement was a position created by one person's thinking. Yet how many other possibilities existed?

In Schrödinger's famous cat illustration, he showed how particles can exist in multiple states, being forced into a position only when they're observed. Our interactions are the same. In any given conversation there are multiple possibilities – an infinite number of outcomes based on what's happening for me, for you, and in the space between. Until we form an opinion, the options are endless; in taking a position, we choose one and make it true.

For Chimamanda Ngozi Adichie, the assumption that all English children drank ginger beer was created by the stories she'd read. This position became her truth, yet just like in the meeting above, the reality was more complex. This is why in human relationships we need to step outside the concept of right or wrong. There is, after all, no universal truth – only our own experience, the other's, and how we relate to each other in the space between.

If this space is the only place we can meet and be in true relationship, then curiosity is the gate. This is because being curious – deeply and genuinely curious about what is happening for us both and why – has the power to correct our experiences of the past. When the times we've felt unheard, talked over, misunderstood, or dehumanised are replaced with just one positive felt experience of someone genuinely wanting to know, the space between us suddenly feels like a safer place to be. In this way, curiosity can be both applied and embodied – more than just something we do, it's something we experience. This is because curiosity activates both the mid-brain (which is responsible for our drive to find things out) *and* the memory-making part of the brain: the hippocampus. When these two areas communicate, we not only learn about others and ourselves, but we *embed* that learning as a memory. This positive felt experience then acts as an antidote to our past, creating psychological safety and allowing us to experience what it's like to be valued and understood – even in organisations where that hasn't been the case before.

THE REAL ROUTE TO EMPATHY

Without curiosity there is no empathy. And yet it seems the organisations that talk about empathy the most are the ones where it's least likely to be taking place. Why?

Christo Brand was a nineteen-year-old prison guard fresh out of training when he was asked to be responsible for a notorious terrorist. Christo knew who this man was, because, like many other young people in his country, he'd been taught about the actions of this monster from a young age. He knew this man as an extremist, a danger to the way of life of his country, an enemy he had learnt to fear.

At first, Christo kept his distance. His role was clear and defined: he simply had to enforce the rules. Yet in time, he noticed that his prisoner wasn't the caricature he'd been taught to expect. He was respectful, even when the system he was imprisoned by treated him with indignity. He also seemed to care deeply about those around him. One day, he started to ask Christo about his life: 'Who are your family?', 'What are your dreams?', 'How do you see the future of your country?' This wasn't small talk – it was a genuine desire to find out about the person he had the least in common with in the world.

As the years went by, Christo also learnt more about his prisoner: his love for his family, his longing to see his children, and the sacrifices he had made for his cause. When Christo's grandson was born, he smuggled the baby in so his prisoner could hold him.

The deep, contagious curiosity the prisoner brought to their relationship allowed Christo to see beyond the single story. It also helped him become curious about what he thought he knew, allowing him to discover the truth behind the label he had grown up hearing. The man was Nelson Mandela, and he would go on to become the first black president of a united South Africa. For Christo Brand, however, he was more than a political giant. He was a grandfather who wanted to hold his grandson.

If we as organisations and teams are serious about building empathy, this is how we must start. Christo Brand didn't have to question his assumptions about Mandela – Mandela's curiosity compelled him to. We must, like Christo, be willing to reject the single story, to allow our thinking to be influenced by the thinking of others. We must set aside the role assigned to us and the beliefs we hold about our circumstances and our past. Only then will we uncover the richness of others' experiences and, in doing so, uncover something greater in ourselves.

Trying to create empathy without curiosity simply forces us into what we think are someone else's emotions. This results in us trying to predict their experience rather than genuinely seeking to understand it. We then make assumptions about how they feel and about the mechanisms behind how they work: *I get that she's overwhelmed. It's because she's new.*

Without being curious enough to find out what is *actually* happening for that person – are they really overwhelmed and, if so, is it really because they're new? – we fail to put ourselves in a position where we can relate to them. Worse, our incorrect beliefs trigger actions: *I'll ask one of the senior members of the team to mentor her. That way she won't feel so overwhelmed.*

This leads to us creating 'solutions' to problems that were never there, all because we failed to ask the question we needed to ask. A result of this might be an employee who feels micromanaged and patronised rather than genuinely heard and understood.

We cannot cultivate empathy by making assumptions about someone's experience. Instead, we must seek to understand their needs, perspectives, and challenges through curiosity, connecting with them in their experience and offering validation and support. In organisations, this has never been more important than now.

RELATIONAL CURIOSITY VERSUS THE NEED TO KNOW

When we understand how curiosity links to empathy, we realise that it isn't just 'finding out'. It's learning what's happening for us, the other, and in the space between, and letting that experience influence our own. This deepens relationships in a way company values can't.

We're all born curious – just look at how a baby follows your movement with its eyes or grabs at your finger. When it's older, that baby will ask 'Why?', then later 'What does that mean?', trying to make sense of how things work and understand the world around it. At its most primal level, this curiosity is linked to our desire to survive – we won't find food, water, shelter, or companionship unless we understand how the world works. Curiosity also activates our dopamine circuitry – the chemical 'reward system' that drives our urge to explore and learn new things. Our brains have evolved to solve complex problems, and we need curiosity to do this.

In organisations, we're also naturally curious. Questions like 'How do we monetise that?', 'How can we reduce costs?', 'How can we get that to market faster?' are about surviving in a world that's fundamentally unpredictable. Changing market forces, customers' fluctuating needs, employees' divergent demands, the generational gap, and the emergence of new technologies all lead us to want to mitigate risk in any way we can. It's why we hire for values such as resilience, adaptability, flexibility, and agility – in the belief that they'll be our weapons against the constant flow of change. We need to increase our grit at the same time as creating cultures of psychological safety, empathy, collaboration, and trust.

Relational curiosity, however – where we allow another's thinking to influence our own – isn't about just finding out.

In fact, it isn't about seeking certainty at all. This is because, rather than measuring systems, data, topics, or trends, it wants to understand people, interactions, relationships, and experiences. This is why relational curiosity is about so much more than knowing what a person thinks – it's about learning their beliefs, their functioning, their values, and their attachment style.

Think about the last time you asked someone 'What do you think?' What was your motivation? Were you asking out of duty because you felt they should be included? Or to blame and shame, gathering ammunition to prove someone else wrong? Perhaps it was so you could get them to agree. Perhaps it was to continue agreeing with yourself.

When we apply and embody curiosity, we allow ourselves to have a different conversation. We open our minds to what we don't know and allow ourselves to empathise, not just on a cognitive level but on a felt one. Only then can we cut through what we *think* we should be asking and instead have one conversation and the right one: 'What happens for you when I say that, and can you share a little more about what that's like?'

BUILDING CURIOSITY IN ORGANISATIONS

To learn how to apply and embody curiosity in our teams and organisations, let's go back to the meeting at the start of this chapter. Imagine if, at the end of that meeting, the conversation had started with this: 'I appreciate we've covered a lot today. Would you mind all sharing a little about what's been happening for you during this meeting?'

Rather than asking if everyone's happy or agrees with what's been said, this open-ended question encourages people to share their experiences. It forces them to reflect, not just on what they think or how they feel, but on what's been happening on a more embodied level. This, as we explored in chapter 3, is the first step to regulation – our ability to notice our nervous system responses then take the elevator up to make sense of them.

When we ask someone 'What's happening for you?', we give them the sense of being seen. When they experience being seen, they're more likely to share their thinking and be open to the thinking of others. This paves the way for reciprocity and relationship within the team, allowing us to truly hear the other person without our own thinking getting in the way. Part of curiosity, then, is regularly asking ourselves, *What's preventing me from hearing this person?* and *What do I need to do to be able to hear them?*

Curiosity is a two-way street. It is dialogue, not monologue, exploring our relationships with uncertainty and sitting with the discomfort of what we do not know. This is why curiosity doesn't start with 'Why?'. When we ask 'Why?', we activate the survival part of the brain, the defence mechanism the other uses to protect them from threat. Rather than stimulating curiosity, this causes them to justify and defend. In asking someone 'Why?', we force them into a position, making it more difficult for them to change their thinking and giving us less chance of finding out what we need to know.

Instead, curiosity begins with open-ended questions. These are questions that invite reflection rather than trying to force someone into a position of a single story. As Adam Grant says, 'The best person to change a person's thinking is themselves.' By asking open-ended questions, we allow the other person to make sense of what's happening in their internal world without the conversation becoming combative or positional.

Here are some examples of open-ended questions that encourage relational curiosity:

- Can you share more about how you got to that decision?
- What informed the way you completed that task?
- Can you tell me more about that?
- Would it be OK if I asked you a couple of questions about...?
- Who else needs to hear this outside this room?
- That sounds really interesting – would you be willing to share more about your thinking on this?

When a team, or person, reflects on and answers these questions, we start to see how they've processed their thinking and responses. We can then quickly understand where they are and whether we're aligned.

In this sense, curiosity can help us hire the right people. When we discover how a person operates rather than simply ticking off company values, we get a clearer picture of who they are. In addition to what they've done, we discover what happens for them in certain situations, how they function, and how they process information and emotions. This means asking questions like:

- How do you learn best?
- What do you do when you come up against something you don't understand?
- How will we know when you need help?
- What benefits do you believe your attributes will bring to both the team and the company?
- What do you find most challenging when working in a team?
- What do you do when something doesn't go to plan?
- If you could ask for one thing from us as a company what would it be?

Open-ended questions also facilitate curiosity in meetings. At the start of a meeting these could be:

- What's the one thing you'd like to get from our time today?
- What about that is important to you?
- What might get in the way of you getting that one thing?
- How will you know when you have got it?

At the end of a meeting, they could be:

- What landed for you today?
- How does that relate to the one thing you wanted to get from today?
- What are you taking away to do?
- What have you learnt about yourself today?
- What have you learnt about us/the team?
- What have you found most challenging?
- What do you personally want to work on as a result of today?

PRACTICES TO SUPPORT CURIOSITY

Like presence and reflection, curiosity starts with leadership. Here are some practical ways to cultivate curiosity in your day-to-day life:

1. Ask permission. Like any principle or process described in this book, curiosity relies on reciprocity and communication. Asking 'Would it be OK if I asked you a question?' slows the pace of the conversation, allows the 'gap' for reflection, and co-regulates your and the other's nervous systems in preparation for something to happen. This allows for vulnerability and brings us back to what we are in service of in the conversation.

2. Find out what is difficult for the other person. For example, eye contact is important for co-regulation, but for the neurologically divergent it might be difficult for them to maintain it or mask their discomfort. The only way to find this out is to ask.
3. Don't presuppose answers. Curiosity means listening to hear rather than listening to confirm, so try to make sense of any biases you might hold about the other person's response.
4. Discard any positions you've arrived at in advance. Curiosity is about moving away from what we think we know and being open to what we don't. This means discarding opinions, beliefs, and assumptions we've arrived at due to past encounters and allowing someone else's thinking to influence ours.

When we allow curiosity in our organisations and teams, we start to let go of our individual opinions, ideas, and assumptions and open ourselves to a different space. This is where creativity and innovation happen and empathy is born, simply because we've learnt to sit with the unknown – the 'messiness' that makes our relationships as humans so rich and unique.

Just because teams are unpredictable doesn't mean they are unmanageable. As humans, we are in fact chaos-capable – each with the capacity to be relational in a way that regulates our own nervous system and helps to regulate those of others. We cannot do this without curiosity. The more curious we are, the more we increase our windows of tolerance for the differences between us, allowing us to collaborate with and understand one another in service of what our organisations want to achieve. Curiosity creates connecting conversations – ones that allow new thoughts, new answers, and new possibilities that were not present in any of us individually.

It's easy to rely on a single story – the narrative we hold about people at the expense of considering anything else to be true. Yet in some senses, we are not a story at all, for a story implies a beginning, a middle, and an end, a 'journey' that progresses and evolves from one point to the next. In creating stories about each other, we try to create a certainty we cannot have. Although the responses and behaviours of our teams cannot be controlled, they can and must be understood – in each interaction, based on experience, through the process of curiosity.

This enables us to step out of the story entirely, going beyond it to the field where there is no right or wrong, but only what is happening for us both. It's only when we reach that space and become curious about what can happen there that our messy relationships become, if not ordered, at least safe.

To do this we must take a risk. We must have the conversation we *need* to have rather than the one we'd prefer to hide behind. This isn't easy, because these conversations are often the very ones that show us what we didn't want to know. So how do we speak to each other with honesty and frankness without creating discord? How do we talk about the things that matter without endangering the relationships we want to build?

In the next chapter, I'm going to show you why this is not just possible, but imperative for an organisation built on trust.

START WITH THIS

Next time you ask a question, pause and ask yourself these questions first:

- Am I listening to hear, or to defend a position I already hold?
- Am I allowing this person's thinking to influence mine?
- Am I willing to be changed by what this person has to say?

Now reflect on what's happening for you. What could be causing you to be defensive? How has this type of questioning gone for you in the past? What biases or assumptions could you be holding about this person? Understanding the intent behind our curiosity is key to building an empathic way to relate to others.

CHAPTER 7

RESPECTFUL CANDOUR – HONEST COMMUNICATION WITH KINDNESS

"For real progress we must have the safety to challenge existing thinking and beliefs."

THE PROBLEM WITH FEEDBACK

In her book *Radical Candor*, Kim Scott talks about creating 'bullshit-free organisations' – workplaces where managers and employees communicate in a direct and unfiltered way. In these organisations, feedback is something not to be feared but to be embraced – given and taken in the spirit of honesty, even if that information is sometimes hard to hear.

What must we do to create this level of candour? As every organisation knows, feedback matters. Yet those who have tried to build a culture of psychological safety will also know how difficult this is. How can we say what we mean in a world where we're all just trying to survive? It's terrifying to work in environments where one wrong word can be interpreted as a personal attack, where well-intentioned feedback is met with suspicion, where the fear of being cancelled or socially ostracised looms over every conversation. The result is that people walk on eggshells, second-guessing their language, their tone – even their facial expressions – because the stakes feel impossibly high. This pressure to avoid offence can be paralysing, silencing the very voices organisations need in order to grow. In these conditions, honest dialogue doesn't just feel risky – it feels dangerous.

Imagine an employee and a manager are having a one-to-one quarterly performance review. The meeting has gone well, and at the end of the session the manager has one final issue to raise. She is nervous about this because she knows the employee might feel defensive. However, the impact of his behaviour on the team is such that she feels her only choice is to speak up. 'Thanks for your time today, David. Before you go, there's just one more issue I wanted to raise. It's to do with the way you come across in meetings.'

'Oh?'

'A few people have told me you tend to dominate the conversation, talking over people, not letting them have their say. I wanted to know if you're aware you were doing that?'

'Um, no, I wasn't. I'm surprised people have said that actually, because I feel I contribute some really great ideas. That's disappointing.'

'Of course, but that's the feedback I'm getting, I'm afraid. To be entirely honest, I've noticed it too. You do talk a lot more than the others, and sometimes I can see that's to the detriment of the team.'

'I don't think that's fair. Everyone gets their say. I can't help being passionate about what I know.'

'I know, it's just that's not how it comes across.'

'OK. Well, I guess I'll tone it down in future, then.'

'Thanks, David. Sorry for bringing it up. I just thought it would be best to clear the air. I'm glad we had this chat.'

'Yeah. Me too.'

As a result of being pulled up on this behaviour, David changed his approach in meetings. He no longer spoke up, withholding his ideas and sitting in silence. His resentment was palpable. Internally, he felt criticised and defensive and also hurt that his colleagues had been complaining about him behind his back. Despite the manager feeling relieved she had 'cleared the air', nothing had been put in place to resolve the issue.

This conversation was certainly candid. It addressed an elephant in the room – a behaviour that needed to be discussed, not least because of the division and gossip happening among other members of the team. Yet despite the manager thinking she'd solved the issue, nothing could have been further from the truth. She had raised it, not resolved it.

When we have honest conversations like this one without applying and embodying relational principles, we become a 'transmitter'. We share necessary information without taking into account what it's for, why we're doing it, or what's happening for us, the other, and in the space between. The result is a conversation that is candid, yet not constructive, that doesn't make room for anyone's thinking to be influenced by anyone else's and doesn't take time for people to make meaning of each other's responses. Rather than creating psychological safety, this kind of 'feedback' pollutes the relational space. It creates a rupture, but without the necessary repair. As a result, we feel attacked and our subsequent survival mode creates discord, mistrust, and alienation – the very things we were trying to avoid.

This is because when the limbic system senses threat (for example, in the form of criticism, control, uncertainty, or unfairness), we will become defensive, attack, or withdraw – in other words, we will enter our survival state.

So does candour have a place in organisations? The answer is yes, yet the kind of candid conversation we most often see is one that causes difficult conversations without the relational processes to see them through. Despite its damaging effect on teams, this is rife. So how are we getting it so wrong?

In giving and receiving feedback, most teams lack one vital ingredient: the psychological safety for individuals to share more than what's on their minds. In other words, they don't pay attention to what's happening for them *beyond words* at the level of their responses and their emotions. In paying attention to the content of what needs to be said, rather than the felt experience of the parties involved, they fail to take into account the meaning behind the behaviour being discussed. In attempting to cure the symptom, they fail to take care of the cause.

Most organisational feedback falls apart because we fail to stop to reflect on the internal experience, fail to get curious about what's happening, and fail to have a conversation about what we can do about it. In most cases, we even fail to assess the person's presence to take part in the conversation at all.

Candour without respect damages teams, prevents collaboration, and erodes relationships of trust. We *think* we're having a difficult conversation when in reality we are only transmitting what we have decided we want to say. In doing so, we create resentment, alienation, and defensiveness without creating a solution to the thing we're trying to address.

THE LONGER, SHORTER WAY

Respectful candour, on the other hand – the giving and receiving of feedback based on presence, reflection, and curiosity in a way that stays true to the giver but also takes into account the emotions of the receiver – is one of life's most challenging skills. It requires us to take a risk: the risk of accepting that our positions might be wrong, the risk of being willing to change our behaviour, and the risk of finding out something we didn't want to know.

Yet with risk comes great reward. By applying and embodying respectful candour in our organisations, we not only demand psychological safety but create it. This is the 'longer, shorter way' – the quickest and easiest route to move from criticism to collaboration without anyone feeling like they're the one to blame. By having one conversation and the *right* conversation, we create the positive felt experience of feedback that does no harm.

Like presence, reflection, and curiosity, respectful candour is a self-fulfilling loop. It isn't the responsibility of one of us but both – co-created in the space between when we're reciprocal in the way we relate to each other. This is because, in any interaction, both parties are equally responsible for how their survival state and attachment styles show up. The benefit of this is that by embodying respectful candour ourselves, we make the space safe for the other to be candid, too.

This can happen almost instantly. Let's see how David's performance review could have gone differently.

'Thanks for your time today, David. Before you go, there's just one more question I wanted to ask. Are you OK to do that now?'

'Yes, sure, I'm all ears.'

'Great. I've noticed lately you have a lot to contribute in meetings. Can you tell me what happens for you when we're all around the table like that?'

'Of course. Well… I guess I have a lot of ideas.'

'Oh, I'd love to hear more about that. What's it like for you when you have an idea you want to share?'

'I get excited, and I really want to tell everyone about it. Sometimes that's a bit frustrating, especially if someone else is talking.'

'That's really interesting. I can see why you might be impatient about that. What's it like for you when you sense that people aren't listening?'

'I feel ignored. Like I'm not appreciated in the team.'

'I see. And what would have to happen for you to not feel like that?'

'I'd need to know people were taking me seriously. That they were considering things genuinely, not just hearing me out.'

'And how would you know that had happened?'

'I guess if I had some kind of feedback. That would show me they'd taken things on board.'

'OK, so, some kind of written or spoken feedback would be useful?'

'Yes.'

'OK, I'll look into that. One more question. I'm wondering if we should think about what happens for the others in the meeting when you share your ideas?'

'Oh. I'd never really thought about that. I guess it might be a bit overwhelming for them. Like I'm talking too much. Now that you mention that, I really get it.'

'David, would you be open to trying something new so you can share your thoughts without people becoming overwhelmed? In the next meeting, perhaps you could share one main idea and then write down the others to send to me afterwards?'

'OK, I think that would work well, actually. It would help me to prioritise the idea I think is the best but also have an outlet for my other thinking, too.'

'Great. Can I ask what's happening for you now, now that we've agreed on that as a solution?'

'I feel a lot calmer, actually. Like I don't need to say everything at once. Thanks, I'm glad we spoke about this.'

What this conversation shows is that while respectful candour requires empathy, it also *creates* it. That's because this kind of honesty – preceded as it is by presence, reflection, and curiosity – is in service *only* of finding out what is happening. Only then can both parties make meaning of their experiences in a way that allows for change.

In this version of the conversation, before being candid with David, the manager asks his permission. Starting with 'Are you OK to do that now?' allows her to check that they're both present enough to give and receive feedback. Then, instead of focusing on David's behaviour, she invites them both to pause and reflect on what's happening for him when he does it: 'What's it like for you when you have an idea you want to share?' This allows for curiosity, not just about David's response but about what might be happening for others: 'I'm wondering if we should think about what happens for the others in the meeting when you share your ideas?'

This shifts the conversation from what is being said to the process of reflection and regulation in order to unpack what might be going wrong. In doing so, they can both co-regulate, taking the elevator up from their emotions to their prefrontal cortices in order to think about their thinking in a more cerebral way. At the basis of this is curiosity: 'Oh, I'd love to hear more about that. What's it like for you when you have an idea you want to share?'

Respectful candour like this is the only way to come out of a difficult conversation with a genuine solution and with relationships intact. In the example above, we can see how quickly this can happen – even in the course of one conversation.

GIVING AND RECEIVING CANDOUR

We often think of candour as something that's given. In reality, the way we receive respectful candour is as important as the way we deliver it. While it's the responsibility of the giver to check if the receiver is available to hear what they have to say, it's also the receiver's responsibility to regulate their response. We can see this if we flip the conversation above on its head. In this version, David is the one applying respectful candour. 'Thanks for your time today, David. Before you go, there's just one more issue I wanted to raise. It's to do with the way you come across in meetings.'

'Oh?'

'A few people have told me you tend to dominate the conversation, talking over people, not letting them have their say. I wanted to know if you're aware you were doing that?'

'Oh, this sounds important enough to raise with me. Can I ask, is this the first time you've noticed this?'

'No, it's been an issue for a while to be honest. For example, at the last brainstorming meeting everyone felt totally overwhelmed by how much you contributed and frustrated by the lack of space for them to talk.'

'I can see why that would be a problem. What was it like for you when people told you that?'

'Well, I was worried to be honest. We've had problems in this team before, and I know how badly things go if we can't collaborate. I could see how this could escalate into something more. It's my job to sort out any discord and I really don't have the time for this.'

'Yep, that makes sense. Are you saying you're worried about whether we can work together as a team?'

'Yes. I can't have unhappy staff. People will leave.'

'I get that. Can I ask – how could I share my ideas in a way that's more in line with what you and the team need?'

'I don't know. Look, I'm always happy to hear the ideas. They're actually great. It's just too much all in one meeting, and then the others don't get a chance to speak. Is there any way you could share your thinking in a more consolidated way?'

'Sure, I can do that. If I then send you my other ideas, perhaps you could share your feedback. Do you think that would work for you and the team?'

'That would be great, actually. I don't want to lose your input.'

'That means a lot. Can I ask – do you feel any different now we've had this conversation?'

'Actually I feel relief. I've been worried about how you'd take this all day. Now I know we've got a real solution.'

This is the opposite of most 'candid' conversations, which happen only at a surface level and fail to reach the depth at which change is catalysed. By pausing to reflect, be present and curious, we not only find a solution to the problem, but give both parties the positive felt experience of what it's like to be heard. When respectful candour is employed – either by the giver or the receiver – the conversation can move easily and quickly to collaboration rather than blame. This can happen even if the giver is 'transmitting', as long as the receiver is curious about what they're trying to say.

CONDITIONS FOR CANDOUR

So why, when respectful candour repairs relationships, strengthens collaboration, and builds empathy among teams, do we often shy away from the conversations we need to have? The answer is once again about risk. Our desire for certainty leads us to avoid any situation in which we might be wrong, judged, or blamed. As a result, we hold on to our beliefs, stay in defence mode, and avoid conversations where we might find out what we don't want to hear.

In candid conversations, this is exactly what we're called to do.

In the 1980s, researchers Robert Blake and Jane Mouton wanted to discover the effect of openness on the functioning of a team. By examining NASA reports on simulated airline accidents, they gained insight into how the relationship between the pilot and crew affected life-and-death decisions. The research revealed that the pilots who were honest with their crews, admitting there was a problem and asking for their advice early on, were more likely to avert disaster than those who didn't share that anything was wrong.

This might not come as a surprise – after all, it's understandable that leaders who ask for the input of the team will be more likely to make an informed decision. However, what's more interesting is what Blake and Mouton discovered about how those pilots interacted with their crews *before* the crash happened. Crew members who had an open, honest, and respectful relationship with their boss in everyday work were more likely to share vital information in an emergency – whether they were asked for it or not. In other words, their psychological safety to share information on the ground meant they were more likely to be honest at the point when it mattered.

This plays out in organisations. In recent research, 85% of employees reported that on at least one occasion they didn't feel they could raise a concern with their managers – even though they felt the information was important.[9] The result might not be a matter of life or death, but it does create teams that are too afraid to have the right conversations at the time they need to have them. This is the essence of a psychologically unsafe organisation: an environment where people don't feel able to share their views without judgement or blame.

So what about boundaries? Can anything be discussed at work?

While we'd all agree there are some topics that aren't appropriate to share, 'boundaries' is a term that has been taken out of context. Rather than using it to describe appropriateness, we've adopted it as an excuse for the barriers we create between ourselves and behaviours we don't want to accept. Yet this ignores a fundamental point: the brain is a relational organ.

We are wired to be in relationship. In fact, our fulfilment and contentment as humans can be found only in the space between us and others. By setting boundaries, we make an individual statement of what we do or do not want, failing to take into consideration what's happening for the other and in the space between. This is a problem because a boundary is a wall. When we build a boundary in the space between, we construct a barrier neither of us can climb. Our relationship then fails to be reciprocal, because while the wall keeps out the behaviour, it also keeps out the chance for regulation, reconnection, and repair.

Respectful candour eliminates the need for this wall. Instead, it helps us have the one conversation – and the right conversation – that allows us to show up effectively in the space between. This opens the way for honest feedback that benefits both the individual and the team.

In other words, when we apply and embody respectful candour, there isn't a conversation we can't have.

BUILDING RESPECTFUL CANDOUR IN ORGANISATIONS

So how do we make space for candid conversations at work?

Of all the principles in this book, I believe respectful candour is the quickest to apply. In fact, it's no exaggeration to say respectful candour can be embedded in your organisation in one interaction. The alternative is slow: avoiding the one, meaningful conversation we need to have in favour of 'workarounds', a lengthy sidestep most organisations can't afford to take.

This is because while psychological safety facilitates these conversations, we don't have to wait for it to exist. Rather, respectful candour *creates* psychological safety – through the felt experience of receiving feedback that does no harm. This can happen surprisingly quickly, even when someone new has joined your team. The good news is that we're all capable of hearing and giving feedback – even challenging feedback – when it's delivered with care and positive intent and we're regulated enough to explore it.

As a giver of feedback, the key is to offer respectful candour *only* when you understand what's happening for you, the other, and in the space between. This is achieved through curiosity. So, rather than launching into your thinking about the product, process, thought, or relationship in question, ask: 'I'm interested in your take on X. Could you share a little bit more about your thinking?' This shows your willingness to forgo traditional models of right and wrong and work together to move forward – in context and in service of what the organisation is trying to achieve. By doing this, you allow the receiver to be heard rather than simply forcing them to listen to a transmission from a giver who neglects to relate to them.

In respectful candour, timing is everything. This means the giver identifying whether the person is available to hear the feedback and checking they're not already in survival mode. In other words, we pick our time for feedback based on the ability of the other to hear it, not on their physical proximity to listen.

Respectful candour is also always in service of a goal. Sharing feedback for the sake of transmission – relaying what we want to say without exploring our need to say it – will always come across as criticism. Instead, respectful candour begins with the giver reflecting on their intentions and establishing what they are in service of as they initiate the conversation. WAIT (Why Am I Talking?) is a useful way to do this, and it can be done both individually and as a team.

Once we know what we're in service of, we can start to use the principles of reflection and curiosity to open the way to a respectfully candid conversation. Our self-questioning might include these questions:

- What's happening for me as I raise this issue?
- Am I willing to hear what the other person has to say?
- How will I let my thinking be influenced by their thinking?
- How can I co-regulate with them in the space between?

By pausing to do this, we embody the values of self-awareness, empathy, reciprocity, and communication. Above all, we understand that the brain is relational: this is not a conversation of 'positions' where I need to get my point across, but rather a meeting taking place outside the concept of right and wrong. Here, we can both be influenced by the other and create a solution that will work.

Language plays a big part in this. When we use absolutes – 'but', 'haven't', 'shouldn't', 'should', 'can't', 'don't', 'won't', 'always', and 'never' – we show our biases through our words. We also stimulate survival mode in the other, disabling their ability to hear and increasing the chance of conflict.

The receiver of feedback has a responsibility, too. By asking the giver what's happening for them, they can help them pause and reflect on their intention. This is true curiosity, as it allows them to be honest with themselves, exploring their position, biases, and assumptions before leaving them at the door. This allows the receiver to regulate with the giver as well as have empathy and compassion for what led them here.

PRACTICES TO SUPPORT RESPECTFUL CANDOUR

Here are some ways of cultivating respectful candour in your day-to-day life:

- Check in to see if the other person is willing to receive feedback. If the situation begins to get heated, pause and suggest you revisit the discussion at another time.
- Be accountable for your own opinions and perspectives. Even if you're not alone in your thinking, take time to reflect on your intentions, biases, and assumptions before you give feedback. If in doubt, ask yourself, *What happens for me as I think about giving this feedback?*
- Avoid giving feedback in a 'sandwich' framework. While a compliment-criticism-compliment structure might seem like a good way of softening the blow, it often makes the compliments seem insincere. Remember: people hear only what comes after the 'but'.
- Ask questions that will lead to a solution. For example, 'What do you think will get in the way of this changing?', 'Who else needs to know this?' and 'How will I know things have improved?'

Respectful candour does not seek to wound. It isn't an excuse to 'let rip', criticise, or speak out of turn. It doesn't dwell on faults, nor is it the giver of empty praise. It doesn't hold positions, support biases, or let our misguided beliefs influence the way we relate to others. It asks a lot of both the receiver and the giver – challenging us to not only communicate with honesty and kindness but to leave our assumptions at the door. It allows thinking to influence thinking, meaning to influence meaning, and what one says about another to influence the way they think about them. Most importantly, it isn't about winning a conversation, but about creating space for dialogue. It says 'Let's talk – not as rivals, but as people who seek to know and be known.'

This requires something more than words. It requires us to risk stepping outside our places of comfort and knowledge and into a space where we are open and exposed. It's only in this place of exposure that we find the security we seek.

START WITH THIS

Next time you need to give feedback, spend some time in preparation. First, bring yourself into presence. Pause. Now write down the *one* thing you want that person to hear. Now ask it in a way that is using curiosity: 'Can you tell me more about...?'

- Are you willing to hear the other person give an answer you didn't think of or expect?

CHAPTER 8

VULNERABILITY - AUTHENTICITY AND OPENNESS

"By embracing mutual vulnerability, we reduce the perceived need for defence or attack responses."

MOVING THE ICE PICK

A few years ago, my good friend Lindsey and I were ice climbing in the Alps when we had to cross a difficult ridge. When we looked down, we were alarmed to see directly below us a huge crevasse. Our guide said that we'd have to cross carefully, using both our crampons and our ice picks to slowly inch across.

Lindsey is utterly fearless. I had no doubt she had the skill to get across, so in the spirit of getting it over and done with, I decided to go first. I picked carefully across the ridge just as the guide had shown me and, with some trepidation, I made it over the crevasse. Then I looked over at Lindsey, who was just starting to make her way across. Suddenly something in her changed. She stopped, her ice picks stuck in the ice, her eyes filled with terror. She had frozen in fear.

I knew in that moment Lindsey was unable to get across that ridge on her own. She was – both figuratively and literally – in survival mode.

After a few seconds, our guide realised that something was wrong and shouted to Lindsey, 'You need to get moving, or the ice may not hold.' Of course, Lindsey knew this, but this sense of urgency not only didn't help, it seemed to increase her fear. She didn't move.

Despite her competency and strength, I could see Lindsey was helpless.

I called across to her. 'Lindsey,' I said, 'look me in the eye'.

'I can't,' she said, her eyes fixed on the ice.

'Yes, you can.'

Her body still frozen, she very slowly turned her eyes to look in my direction.

'OK, Lindsey, I'm going to help you,' I said. 'I'm going to pick up the ice pick in my right hand, and I'm going to place it a metre away from me to the right – like this. I need you to do the same.'

'I can't.'

'Pick it up right now,' I said. 'On three, OK? One, two, three, let's go.'

Keeping my eyes on her, I exaggeratedly moved my ice pick a metre to the right. Slowly and with trembling hands, she copied. I then moved the pick in my left hand to the right, showing her she had to do the same. She did. For the next few minutes we continued like this – step by step, pick by pick – until she was eventually able to get across the crevasse.

Afterwards, Lindsey and I reflected on this experience. We were, thankfully, able to laugh about it. Lindsey said she didn't know what had happened, she had just suddenly experienced this deep-rooted fear.

I said, 'It's only because I know you so well I was able to see how scared you were.'

She said, 'It's only because I know *you* so well I was able to accept your help.'

A FAILURE TO FAIL

No matter how capable, professional, or skilled we are at our jobs, we all experience moments of vulnerability. And though we try to hide it, our fear has a way of slipping through.

It manifests as micromanagement, aggression, unhealthy competition, avoidance of feedback, lack of trust. Whatever the outward behaviour, the root cause is the same: we're in survival mode.

The problem is that we've spent so much time proving our competence – our ability, dependability, and strength – that we do everything we can to suppress that fear. In the process, we cling desperately to what we think we know. Like Lindsey, we freeze.

We're stuck in the ice.

What we fear most is failure. From an early age, we're taught to avoid it at all costs. It's ingrained in us, shaping how we think and act. We procrastinate, evade, bluff, cover up, deny – all in an effort to escape failure. We grow up learning the value of being right, strong, certain, and capable. We mitigate risk because risk means there's a chance we might fail. Nowhere is this more apparent than in organisations and teams.

When Brené Brown gave her now-famous 2010 TED Talk, 'The Power of Vulnerability', she asked people to share what made them vulnerable. The most common answers were:

- Being turned down or rejected
- Public speaking
- Apologising
- Telling someone you're struggling
- Admitting a lack of knowledge
- Asking for help
- Giving or receiving feedback
- Sharing creative work
- Admitting you got it wrong

The reason these were the most common answers – and the reason you recognise them yourself – is that they are universal truths. They happen everywhere, to everyone, in all walks of life. And yet, in most organisations, showing vulnerability in these challenges is exactly what we avoid. Instead, we turn our fear into something else: defence. We might say:

- 'The CEO got it wrong.'
- 'How could I be expected to know?'
- 'I told you my workload was too much.'
- 'It wasn't my fault.'

Instead of admitting our vulnerability, we use it to blame and shame others, replacing the pain of perceived weakness with a position of attack. If we've developed an avoidant attachment style, we might withdraw completely. Either way, we're stuck: afraid to step back from our positions because we've invested so much in them, yet unable to move forward because we're too frightened to move. Why?

Because vulnerability is *terrifying*.

Being vulnerable at work exposes the soft parts of ourselves we'd rather people didn't see. Here we are, in a position we fought to get to, having to admit 'I can't do that, I need help.' Our fear of vulnerability isn't always articulated, of course, or even conscious. Rather, it *happens* within us, physically and in an embodied way, as a felt experience of what happened in the past. For example, if we were ridiculed or punished or felt a deep sense of shame for our mistakes, we may have subsequently learnt to associate failure with inadequacy. This leads us to avoid trial and error, shun vulnerability, and mitigate risk. We'll then relate to the people around us only on a surface level because finding deeper meaning is just too frightening.

As a result, our conversations are often in vain. We talk in circles, failing to find the solutions we need. This is because without vulnerability we struggle to be meaningfully present, struggle to reflect on what is happening, struggle to be curious, and struggle to be respectfully candid. In fact, until we're willing to explore our relationships with failure – not only the way we process mistakes but the meaning we assign to the experience of making them – we will find it hard to engage with each other at all.

For Lindsey, getting across the crevasse required her to reveal her vulnerability. She then had to trust me, not only accepting she was vulnerable, but *experiencing* with me how that felt. On my part, I had to see her fear. That meant being present, reflecting on what was happening, and being willing to step alongside her to navigate across. It wasn't the fact that I didn't also feel vulnerable that allowed me to help her across, but rather that I had learnt in my body how to engage with that experience. As a result, I knew what vulnerability was like and I was able to be with Lindsey in that moment.

Without admitting to and leaning into our own vulnerability, we'll not only struggle to find a solution to our fear, we'll also fail to enter the relationships we could have if only we let ourselves be changed.

This is because there's another reason we see vulnerability as so deeply dangerous: as well as admitting what we cannot *do*, it means admitting what we do not *know*.

VULNERABILITY AS A GATEWAY TO CHANGE

The reason so many of us are stuck in survival mode – like Lindsey, frozen with fear, unable to move forwards across the crevasse – is that it feels strangely safe. After all, our long-held beliefs, stories, and biases form part of our identities

– even the ones that aren't true. Letting go of them means taking a step into what we don't know. This is why so many organisations and teams and the people within them lack vulnerability: not only do we fear *getting* it wrong, we fear *being* wrong.

Vulnerability is frightening because it forces us to confront something: our survival state, our attachment styles, our beliefs, and the stories we maintain in our desire to feel safe. Without these, we feel exposed because in letting go of our thinking we open ourselves to the possibility of having to do what we do not want to do: change.

The problem with this is that holding on to certainty is a bigger threat to effective teams and organisations than letting go. By refusing to be vulnerable, we fail to open ourselves to another way of being. We rely solely on our instrumental brain – the part of the brain that is interested in getting things done. The instrumental brain doesn't allow others to sense our vulnerability or know how much we care. It engages in logic, justification, anger, blame and shame, grievances, and explanations. More than missing out on the creativity, connection, and collaboration that come from being vulnerable, we create silos, politics, dogma, and cliques. Like Lindsey, what we're clinging to is just as dangerous as what we're trying to escape.

A willingness to be wrong is at the heart of any empathic and psychologically safe organisation. As Brené Brown said, 'Vulnerability is the first thing I look for in you and the last thing I'm willing to show you.'[10] This is because vulnerability is more than admitting what we find hard. It's managing emotional risk, having the courage to share our thinking, and exploring and growing as a result of what we're willing to set down. In other words, vulnerability isn't just disclosing a perceived weakness; it's accepting how to deal with uncertainty.

I was working with a brilliant designer called Will when I started to notice he didn't deal well with praise. Whenever I complimented him, he would play it down, saying things like 'I could have done it better with more time' or 'It wasn't as good as I'd have liked.'

One day I said, 'Will, I'm curious – what happens for you when someone gives you praise?'

He thought for a minute. 'I feel uncomfortable.'

I nodded. 'Can you tell me more about what that's like?'

'Well, my chest feels tight. I struggle to look them in the eye. It makes me just want to run away.'

I reflected on this for a minute, then I asked, 'When you hear someone praise you, what does that change for you?'

He thought for a long time, then he said, 'I guess it means I've succeeded. And that's not me. I've always been the one who's had to try harder, do better, keep improving. That's how it was at school. I was never enough.'

'I really hear you felt you weren't enough,' I said. 'What would accepting praise mean you'd have to do differently?'

'It would mean just being me, I guess. But if I'm honest, I don't really know who that is.'

True vulnerability asks something of us. That might be a question – 'What now?' or 'Who are you?' – or it might be to see something differently. It might challenge us to deepen a relationship, alter our thinking about a person we don't like, or change the dynamic with a person we do. By asking Will to reflect on what happened for him when he received praise, I allowed him to show up with me in the space between us to make meaning of that response. Through respectful candour and curiosity, I showed him there was value in being vulnerable – as long as I was, too.

BRINGING YOUR WHOLE SELF TO WORK

For some people, being vulnerable at work feels deeply unnatural. For others, it's part of the way they are. This is especially true for younger generations, particularly the eighteen-to-thirty-year-olds currently entering the workforce. For them, full emotional disclosure is the defining characteristic of their generation. They've grown up being told it's 'OK to not be OK', encouraged to share their internal experiences and be open without shame. They demand not only to bring their whole selves to work, but to be handled with care.

So why does their natural willingness to be vulnerable so often backfire?

While, in theory, bringing these vulnerabilities, fears, longings, losses, hopes, desires, and fragilities into the workplace is a good thing, the reality is not so straightforward. This is because when Gen Zers bring their whole selves to work, they often clash with the people who are already there. These are Gen X and baby boomers – people who grew up in the '70s and '80s and now make up the majority of senior management. For them, expressing emotion has little place at home, let alone in the workplace. As a result, Gen Z's emotional openness feels nothing more than attention-seeking indulgence. Whether it's requests for reasonable adjustments, 'playing the mental health card', or absenteeism due to anxiety, many of these older workers respond to Gen Z's perceived lack of resilience with a collective eye roll. It's no surprise, then, that in organisations where three, four, or five generations work together, generational bias is a threat to the team. In fact, this conflict has become so intense, some companies are rethinking their hiring decisions completely. In 2024, 30% of companies who employed Gen Zers said they'd never do so again.[11]

Given that by 2030 Gen Z will make up 30% of the workforce, this isn't a sustainable position. So how do we tackle the clash of generations when one wants to be vulnerable while the other doesn't want to know?

The first challenge when Gen Zers bring their whole selves to work is that the people the 'self' is being brought to have absolutely no clue what to do with it. The second challenge is that neither do they. While Gen Z have been taught to express their emotions, they've also been given the wrong language to do it. Pseudo-psychological terms such as 'toxic', 'gaslighting', 'narcissist', 'triggered', 'boundaries', 'antisocial', 'depression', 'anxiety', 'stress', and 'burnout' might be descriptions of how they feel, but they are still left fundamentally unheard. They've also been taught that their feelings are caused by others. In reality, no one 'makes' us feel anything. We feel what we feel as a result of the way we process information and stimuli – much, if not almost all, of which was bedded down in our early lives. Our responses are not caused by others, but are a result of our experiences in the past.

The answer, as always, is beyond words. It is noticing what is happening for us, the other, and in the space between and making meaning so we can correct that experience. When a young person reveals their vulnerabilities to a team not ready to receive them, their desire to be heard isn't met. This results in them either shouting louder in a desperate attempt to be rescued or withdrawing by taking a mental health day, all while the older generation become more irritated by their drama, more resentful of their entitlement, and plunged deeper into their own survival state. The result is that both parties fail to be heard, both fail to co-regulate, and both fail to relate to each other in the space between.

RESPONSE AND RESPONSIBILITY

The beautiful thing about the moment of vulnerability I experienced with Lindsey was that she was not dumping her fear on me in a desire to be saved; her fear was a barrier to what we had to achieve. Overcoming it together was in her interests and in mine.

In many organisations where vulnerability has been encouraged, however, we've forgotten our collective goal. Bringing your whole self to work without knowing what that self is in service of will always end in a failure to relate to your colleagues. This is because, just as we cannot show up in the space between us without presence, reflection, and curiosity, we cannot show up somewhere where someone has dumped their stuff.

This is where we can talk about sharing our emotions only with a sense of context. With vulnerability comes responsibility – if we bring our personal challenges to work, we must consider the impact of that on others and the space between. Just as importantly, we must work out how it affects our ability to get things done. Accepting this responsibility changes everything. It forces us to be more considered in our vulnerability, taking us from response to thinking, thinking to curiosity, and curiosity to finding out what the other person needs from us to do their job.

This comes back to process over content – considering our *experiences* of the conversation instead of what the conversation is about. In this sense, true vulnerability is less about sharing a personal problem and more about sharing what happens for us in our interactions with others. Then we can be open about our challenges, our survival state, and our attachment styles because we're both in service of what the team is trying to do.

Embracing this level of responsibility alongside transparency and authenticity allows each individual to feel valued rather than overwhelmed. This is the true sense of 'bringing your whole self to work'.

For this we need to apply and embody the other principles and practices: monitoring our presence, regulating our responses, being curious enough to create empathy, and having the one right conversation in a spirit of respectful candour. We then create a psychologically safe environment that shifts from tension and anxiety to each of us being able to show up without fear.

The reciprocal nature of vulnerability is important here. I help you experience being comfortable with your vulnerability – I move my ice pick so you can move yours – and you need to understand that what you share has an impact on me. This is not a limitation, but rather an opportunity, as it's only through vulnerability that we create the positive felt experience of working in a trusted team. This is particularly valuable in uncertain or high-stakes conversations, as it replaces the need for self-protection with small, intentional steps towards a relationship of trust.

I've seen this happen first-hand. I was working with a relatively new team who had had to 'hit the ground running' on a high-stakes project. As a result, they hadn't spent any real time understanding the company's vision. Alongside the company director, I created a workshop where he could share the vision and get feedback on how the team felt.

While the director was sharing the vision on a whiteboard, I looked around the room. I could see a mixture of responses, so as soon as he finished, I asked everyone the following question: 'What's been happening for you as you see the vision up there in black and white?'

One by one they began to share. The first person said, 'It seems like a real challenge. I feel slightly overwhelmed, but also excited.'

The second said, 'I found it terrifying. All I can think of is how much it relies on me hitting my numbers.'

A third shared, 'I feel really reassured. I'm happy with the timeline and I think we can get it done.'

Then a fourth person spoke up. 'I feel quite resentful, actually. It seems like we're going to do all the work here, but another department is going to piggyback on it to make all the profit. It doesn't seem fair.'

As I looked around the room, I was interested to see a lot of people nodding at this last statement. I realised that this was what I needed to pay attention to – because it was the most vulnerable of the responses and because it clearly expressed a need: to be valued and remunerated for the hard work the team would have to do.

I paused the discussion. 'How will you know, as a team, that you're being valued in this? What would that look like in practical terms?'

The discussion continued, and the team agreed they wanted a separate discussion with the director around compensation and the distribution of profits, as well as visible recognition in front of the other teams, the organisation, and the client for what they had achieved. That way they'd know they were valued enough to be rewarded for their work.

In offering space to explore this question – a question that was candid, reflective, curious, and in service of a goal – the team was able to come up with a clear solution. They didn't get stuck in their emotions about the vision, because, by noticing and naming them, they'd taken the elevator up to think about what they meant. They were then able to come up with smart ideas about how they could feel valued by the rest of the organisation.

Without vulnerability, these emotions might have been acted out in a different way. There might have been unspoken resistance to working collaboratively, the withholding of information, deep-seated anxiety about performance, the micromanaging of junior staff, stress about hold-ups and delays, attempts to claim territory and credit. Now it was all named, however, we were able to move on from that discussion and get on with the rest of the work, all because we'd got out of where we were stuck together.

BUILDING VULNERABILITY IN ORGANISATIONS

Like respectful candour, facilitating vulnerability is about slowing down to speed up. Every person is an imperfect human and the world is an imperfect place – it's why teams, by their nature, are imperfect. To improve the wellbeing and relational capacity of our teams, however, we must begin with the thing we least want to do: take risks. This means being prepared to fail, employing trial and error, even accepting rupture and conflict – anything that increases our windows of tolerance for uncomfortable experiences. The team that wins is not the team that makes the fewest mistakes, after all, but the team that sits in uncertainty with confidence rather than fear.

It's important to note that encouraging vulnerability at work is just the beginning. When attachment styles are uncovered, this might prompt the need for individuals to do work off-site – either with a therapist or with a psychologist – to make meaning of their vulnerabilities and help them show up better in the team. It is not a manager's job to fix their employees. Their job is facilitating a safe space where meaning can be made through noticing what's happening, regulating the response, and taking the elevator up to a more cerebral place. With curiosity and respectful candour, we can then sit comfortably in the discomfort of vulnerability without the need to take a position of defence.

One way of doing this is to focus on the *process* of the disclosure rather than the information itself. So, instead of 'What should I reveal?', we ask 'What is the source of this impulse?' Is it a personal need, a desire to share? In this case, it serves only the discloser. Or is it a collective process for the purpose of the group? In this sense, true vulnerability is the responsibility of the sharer *and* the recipient, so they can both co-regulate in the space between.

We should also always ask permission to disclose. This can be as simple as saying 'I hear you're asking me about X. Would it be OK if I shared my experience?' This helps the other prepare their system and check in to see whether they're available and attuned to hear what you're about to share. In other words, we have to go down to the place of what is happening for them, how they function, and how they process information as a way to understand what needs to happen for the common good.

In many cases, vulnerability needs to be invited – explicitly and open-endedly. This shows that, as well as sharing your own experience, you're open for others to share theirs. Some questions that facilitate this are:

- I'd really like to know – what's your thinking on this?
- How can I help?
- What's happening for you as we talk about this?
- What happened for you in the past when you did that?

As psychological safety expert Amy Edmondson puts it: 'To create safety, leaders need to actively invite input. It's really hard for people to raise their hands and say, "I have something tentative to say", but it is equally hard for people not to answer a genuine question from a leader who asks for their opinion and help.'

PRACTICES TO SUPPORT VULNERABILITY

As a leader, when you share your own challenges and mistakes, you establish the psychological safety needed for others to share theirs. This prevents these vulnerabilities hiding in the shadows and acting out at times when you need a resilient, collaborative team. By establishing the correct conditions for vulnerability now, you'll have a trusted team when you need it most.

Here are some specific ways you can increase vulnerability in meetings and one-to-ones:

- Show your vulnerability early on. Reflect on the areas you are not skilled at and practise asking the team for help, getting comfortable with phrases like 'What do you think?', 'This isn't my area of expertise so I'd value your thinking on it', and 'I know you're skilled in this area. What do you think I might be missing right now?'
- Acknowledge discomfort. One reason leaders fail to invite vulnerability is the fear of not being able to manage the information being disclosed. Noticing this and regulating your response will help people feel safe enough to bring their whole selves to work in a healthy way. One way of doing this is to ask 'What do you need from me most right now – for me to listen or to comment?' We then know our roles in relation to the vulnerability, allowing us to regulate our responses in service of the conversation.

- Be willing to seek a solution. Revealing vulnerability must be in service of a shared goal, so get used to monitoring what you're willing to share and checking you have the capacity to invite change. This can be in the form of questions like 'Who else needs to hear this?' or 'Who do you think would be best placed to help you with this?'
- Name the emotional experience. The best way to notice what's happening for us as we experience vulnerability is to name it. Only then can we take the elevator up to process that experience cognitively.
- Choose the right language. This centres the conversation on what is *happening* rather than what you believe the other is 'causing' you to experience. For example, instead of 'You never listen to me', say 'I notice I feel unheard in meetings and I want to understand how we can shift that.' Remember: no one makes you feel anything.
- When faced with a problem, don't rush to a solution. Instead, go around the room and ask 'What's it like for you to not have the answer?' This gives people the opportunity to become comfortable with not knowing, which in turn reveals vulnerability both individually and collectively. It also allows the team to reflect together on what they need to pay attention to in order to move the issue forward. Other questions you can ask when looking for solutions include:
  - What's the one thing you want me to hear?
  - What do you need most from me right now?
  - What do you feel would be the best way forward? What might be getting in the way of us doing that?

Vulnerability goes beyond sharing personal weakness. It involves a willingness to admit how our own attachment styles or survival state might be affecting what happens for us, the other, and in the space between. When we're open about these aspects of ourselves, we create an opportunity for our teams to support us in addressing these challenges – not by rescuing us, but by moving their ice picks to help us move ours. True vulnerability isn't about evading responsibility or asking for a way out because something is hard. It's in service of finding an effective way forward, one that encourages us to take risks at the same time as acknowledging our fear.

Doing that together – through reflection, curiosity, respectful candour, and vulnerability – opens an opportunity in even the most diverse of organisations to relate to other people on a level beyond words. When we do this, it doesn't matter how different we are – we find a way to get along.

The result is an organisation where difference is not just accepted, but becomes a fundamental ingredient in the way we relate to each other. In the next chapter, we'll see how this is done – and why you'll never need another Diversity, Equity and Inclusion (DEI) initiative again.

START WITH THIS

One of the best ways to lean into vulnerability is to sit in the discomfort of not knowing. In the next week, seek out a conversation with someone around a topic you know nothing about. Once you've had the conversation, take time to reflect on and be curious about the following questions (you could even write the answers down):

- How does this challenge your own thinking?
- What differences do you notice?
- What happens for you when you do not know?
- What might have happened in the past to make this uncomfortable for you?
- How would being vulnerable here change what you think about yourself?

CHAPTER 9

NAVIGATING DIFFERENCE – EMBRACING DIVERSITY

"Our collective capabilities exceed the sum of individual contributors."

BEYOND THE DEI PROMISE

In May 2020, the death of George Floyd at the hands of a white Minneapolis police officer triggered anti-racism protests worldwide. Up to 26 million people participated in Black Lives Matter rallies across the US alone, making it one of the largest protest movements in the country's history.

Businesses, non-profit organisations, and governments duly doubled down with the words of Edmund Burke ringing in their ears: 'The only thing necessary for the triumph of evil is for good men to do nothing.' Staying silent wasn't an option.

Organisations big and small were forced to confront their hiring processes, hierarchies, and institutions for inequality – not just racial but across diversity of all kinds. They rushed to release statements, launch DEI initiatives, and hire 'chief diversity officers'. Yet just five years later, nothing seems to have changed. The unemployment rate among Black Americans is still almost twice that of white Americans, while 69% of individuals from ethnic minorities in the UK report experiencing some form of discrimination at work.[12] In February 2025, Google announced it was reviewing its DEI initiatives and scrapping its diversity-based hiring targets for good.[13]

Why, just five years after the scramble to include people of all backgrounds in organisations, is the DEI movement already dead?

One opinion is that many organisations responded in a purely performative way. A blacked-out social media post here, a nod to neurodiversity there, their actions seemed designed to virtue-signal rather than address systemic issues.

Yet even for those who took DEI seriously – tackling hiring biases, pay gaps, and issues in workplace culture, for example – interest has quickly waned. Financial pressures, increased bureaucracy, and cultural fear of getting it wrong have led employees and leaders alike to realise that this approach doesn't work. In the worst cases, far from leading to better inclusion, DEI seemed to create more discomfort, more defensiveness, and more polarisation than ever before.

The real reason diversity initiatives fail has little to do with racism, sexism, ageism, or homophobia. Instead, it's linked to our fundamental failure to navigate difference. By rolling out initiatives, setting quotas, and promoting inclusion, organisations forgot one thing: a workplace that's successfully diverse isn't the same as a workplace that's successfully different.

As humans, our differences are not as linked to our identities and cultures as we think. Rather, they lie in the way we relate to each other: our communication styles, our values, our autonomic responses, and our thinking. Our failure to understand this is why, as Johnny Taylor, CEO of the Society for Human Resource Management, put it, 'While most workplaces are significantly more diverse than they were twenty years ago, they're also more divided.'[14]

GENDER AND GENERATION

For decades – maybe even centuries – the workplace was dominated by men. A characteristic of this was a working style based on strength, stoicism, rationality, and competition and devoid of compassion and vulnerability. 'I can do it,' we said, 'no problems here.'

As a result, in the name of professionalism and getting ahead, this cohort were not taught to regulate their emotions. Their autonomic nervous system responses were either shut down, dysregulated, and suppressed in the name of getting on with the job or allowed to explode in the form of anger and attack.

Then, in the 1980s and '90s, workplaces became more diverse. Women stepped not only into the meeting room but into leadership, bringing with them a different way of working entirely. This shift was, of course, a positive thing. It led to greater emotional intelligence, more vulnerability, the chance for psychological safety, and a more balanced approach to decision-making. Yet it also created challenges: increased sensitivity, political correctness, tiptoeing around language, and the potential to cause offence.

The divide between the sexes had never been greater.

In the last decade we've seen a similar shift, this time not between the sexes but between the generations. As baby boomers work longer before retiring and Gen Z enters the workforce for the first time, generational diversity is at an all-time high. As we've seen, the older generations have found this hard. They weren't given the tools to notice, name, and make meaning of their emotions, let alone the emotions of others. As a result, instead of regulating, reflecting, asking, and revealing, they tend to railroad, misunderstand, talk over, and dismiss.

The point about diversity is that while these two tensions come from different sources, the foundational issue is the same. Our incapacity to relate to others comes not from differences in our *identities* but from differences in how we sense, feel, communicate, and connect.

This is relational poverty – the growing disconnection between people in the workplace. It stems not only from the colour of someone's skin, their sex, or their age, but from their failure to relate to others in the space between. This is why DEI initiatives have not worked. When we are forced to be inclusive, members of the workforce become fearful they will get it wrong. The phrase 'I'm offended' becomes the most feared statement in the workplace, because as soon as it is uttered the emotion of offence takes all the power. The stakes in this are so high – at best we might be cancelled, at worst we could be dismissed – that instead of supporting connection and understanding others, we retreat to our state of survival. The result is that nobody feels they can be themselves, everyone has to always agree, they try to use the same language, and they spend much of their time avoiding offence. Without being *relational*, DEI initiatives will not only fail – they'll cause the opposite of what they're trying to create.

To avoid workplaces that are fragile, where people are quick to take offence, slow to listen, and unable to steer through tension and conflict as positive felt experiences, we must find the missing piece. That means first acknowledging diversity and then actively engaging with it to co-create a safe space where we can relate to each other. Then our diverse thoughts, experiences, and perspectives aren't a problem to be solved, but an opportunity to build resilience, relational capacity, and an expanded window of tolerance for difference.

UNEXPECTED INPUTS

Why do we find navigating difference so difficult? It's all to do with the signals the brain receives.

In its role of keeping us safe, the brain acknowledges that what we don't know is more likely to be dangerous than what we do. As a result, it amplifies unexpected sensory inputs over predictable ones, making events we find unfamiliar stand out.[15] In teams and organisations, this has a particular effect. When someone has a different background, culture, or even opinion to us, the brain treats it as an unexpected input and sets off an alert.

This is normal. If this experience of the unknown proves to be safe – for example, by the other showing signals of their own system being regulated – our brains 'stand down', regulating their responses and returning to normal. If our experiences of difference don't feel safe, however – through signals of aggression, defensiveness, or criticism – our systems automatically activate their defences. Not only this, but they remain on even higher alert for unexpected inputs in the future. This is why ruptures caused by difference are so damaging when they're not repaired – the pattern continues in a perpetual state, usually culminating in someone leaving the job, changing department, or in some way avoiding the unexpected input they've been forced to face. When we come out of our survival state and hold a mindset of abundance, however, we begin to see how alike we are. Far from being divided by our differences, we are all fearful, we all want to belong, and we all want to be valuable and valued.

In organisations rife with relational poverty, however, we're too caught in our survival state to see it. This is exacerbated by the fact that division and hate are deeply embedded in our culture – we only need to look at political debate or social media to prove it. Our world has become so deeply polarised we've created an almost visible split between woke and anti-woke: on one side are those who are outraged and on the other are those who mock the outrage.

Once again, at the heart of this struggle to navigate difference is a fundamental misunderstanding of how our brains and bodies respond – of our survival state and attachment styles, the autonomic responses that play such a powerful role in shaping how we react when faced with perspectives or experiences that challenge our own. This is what pushes us into defensive postures – the fight, flight, freeze, or fawn states that make it impossible for us to hear.

Our attachment styles also play a major role in how we approach difference. An anxious attachment style, for example, might make us overly focused on others' approval, leading to people-pleasing, overtalking, or resentful compromise. An avoidant style may lead to us retreating from difference altogether, preferring to dismiss or devalue other perspectives rather than risk engaging with something unknown.

These patterns create defensive filters, often manifesting as judgement, dismissal, or avoidance. The 'other' feels too different, the change feels too hard, our biases are too ingrained. Without addressing these survival-driven tendencies, navigating difference becomes almost impossible.

NETWORKS VERSUS COMMUNITIES

When we fail to engage with difference effectively, we fail to meet people where they are. This leads to diverse perspectives being ignored or suppressed and people feeling ultimately unheard or misunderstood. The result – breakdowns in relationships, resentment, high staff turnover, disengaged employees, lost opportunities for innovation – aren't just damaging for individual mental health, they're damaging for the organisation itself.

I was once working with a sales director who had just taken a job in a start-up. Having worked all his life in banks and large corporates, he shared with me how challenging he found working in such a diverse team. Unlike his previous workplaces, where everyone had similar goals, mindsets, and KPIs focused on money, these people came from different industries, thought differently, and were at different stages in their careers.

He and the COO had created a set of KPIs they believed would drive performance and collaboration. However, instead of improving results, the new metrics had so far had no positive impact.

'I can't understand why the team isn't pulling together,' he told me. 'Aren't we all ultimately after the same thing?'

I asked him, 'What *are* they after?'

'What do you mean?'

'Well, what drives each person in your sales team?'

'I don't know.'

'Can I ask another question?' I said. He nodded. 'How does each of those people work best?'

Again, he admitted, 'I don't know.'

Through the conversation that followed, the sales director began to see that the KPIs he and the COO had created were based on assumptions, not actual knowledge of their team's needs, values, and work styles. Not only this, but the company's recruitment process was focused only on skills and qualifications, rather than on understanding how potential hires processed information, engaged with others, and approached their work.

Without this deeper awareness, he had been leading with a one-size-fits-all mindset in a workplace where people were very different.

To navigate difference, we must shift our focus from changing minds to changing how we engage with and process the unknown. We cannot do this unless we understand what motivates people.

It's no secret that social media has made this difficult. Instead of communities made up of different people with different experiences of the world, we now exist in networks – fluid, transient groups of similar people where we can curate our surroundings to reflect what we already believe. If at any point we stop agreeing, we can simply remove ourselves from the group.

In the workplace, however, we cannot block, mute, disconnect, or remove. We must coexist even when we disagree. Yet our ability to silence people online has fuelled a culture where we're less equipped to sit in the discomfort of difference. As a result, we're unwilling to relate to each other and powerless to hear another point of view.

If we're to build workplaces that thrive, we must avoid creating 'networks' of like-minded people. All these do is reduce our windows of tolerance for difference. Instead, we must relearn what it feels like to be safe in an environment where we're not all the same – and stay connected even when our views happen to differ.

Making difference non-threatening is all about how our systems perceive it. After all, it's not the difference itself that puts us in survival mode, but our perception of how dangerous it is. Whether the unexpected input feels safe or not depends on our experiences of how it appears. This is governed by our ability not only to navigate difference, but to apply and embody all the principles in this book. Here's what I mean.

What if next time you encounter a difference in opinion that offends you, you focused not on how much you disagree but on your ability to be **present** enough to truly hear? What if then, instead of moving into survival mode, you **reflected** on what is happening for you, the other, and in the space between? Imagine you then allowed yourself to become **curious** about what your response might mean and what could be informing the response of the other? And imagine that led to you accepting your own **vulnerability** in your response and being **respectfully candid** enough to ask a real question: 'What's the most important thing you want me to hear right now? And are you open to hearing a different thought?'

BEYOND DEI

It's important to note that this process doesn't prevent conflict. Instead, it uses the positive *experience* of conflict as an antidote to the times when disagreement felt unsafe. This allows our systems to learn a different way – recognising not only that difference is OK, but that it can be an opportunity to learn, innovate, collaborate, and connect.

This is not about DEI. It's about the application and embodiment of a way of relating. It can be employed across organisations and teams made up of differences of any kind – from the varied perspectives of stakeholders to the differing needs of customer and supplier. It can help you transform recruitment, meetings, teams, and partnerships – no matter who's taking part and what's happened in the past. This all happens because we stop focusing on the difference itself and start paying attention to how we navigate it, helping us to stop polarising who we are and start connecting with how we respond.

It might not surprise you that in my work with organisations I rarely get into conversations about DEI. This is because navigating difference is about addressing relational poverty, not focusing on whichever catchy term is popular or which movement is happening at the time. Being relational asks us to step away from what divides us, not towards it. That's not to say we don't need to understand different ethnicities, generations, genders, sexualities, neurodiversities, and socioeconomic backgrounds. We do. After all, it's context that explains conduct. Yet we do this only in service of understanding how those experiences have shaped how we relate to one another, not to highlight the difference itself. When we become curious about how we work, the particular difference we're navigating becomes irrelevant: we simply join that person in the space between.

BEYOND THE SHIRT

When we focus on what we have in common rather than our differences, community takes on a different meaning. We no longer belong to a group defined by our sex, race, background, or beliefs, but rather one made up of human beings with a shared goal. By highlighting what we can do together, rather than creating separate spaces for different groups, we're able to navigate difference in a more powerful way.

In 2005, researcher Mark Levine carried out an experiment to see how this works. A group of football supporters encountered a stranger who appeared to trip and injure themselves. The study found the fans were far less likely to help the stranger if they were wearing the shirt of a rival team than if they were dressed in the strip of their own clubs. The researchers then conducted a second experiment. This time, the injured stranger wore a shirt that was neutral, identifying them as a football fan but not affiliating them to a particular team. The results were astonishingly different. When the fans viewed the stranger only as a fellow lover of football, they were more likely to help them get back on their feet – even without knowing which team they supported.

To successfully navigate difference, we must get beneath the shirt. This includes stepping away from ideologies like sexism, racism, ageism, ableism, homophobia, and transphobia – the 'isms' which have a habit of being in service of nothing but themselves. Instead, we must find respect for difference in a place beyond markers of identity, race, gender, and religion. We must consider how people are attached, how they communicate, and how they make meaning of the experiences they've had. In order to know someone, I must connect *all* the dots – not just who that person is, but what happens for them as they navigate life.

Disagreement is not a threat. In fact, according to Ed Tronick, we spend most of our time relationally 'mismatching'. After all, we each have a unique set of experiences, characteristics, skills, and aptitudes, and it's in our nature to see things differently. The key, as ever, is not in the rupture, but in the repair. Our ability to traverse the mismatch, create a positive, corrective experience, and increase our windows of tolerance for the unknown is what dictates our development of trust. When we navigate difference with curiosity, regulation, vulnerability, and candour, over time our relational ruptures become less of a threat.

BUILDING NAVIGATING DIFFERENCE IN ORGANSATIONS

So how do we rewrite the conversation about difference in our organisations and teams?

It all starts with self- and co-regulation. By noticing and naming our experiences, we can prevent survival mode and take the elevator up to make meaning of them through our thinking. When we focus on this process rather than the content of the conversation, the person we're in relationship with is less likely to take offence, less likely to react, and less likely to enter survival mode. This allows us both to step out of our positions and into the space between, increasing our ability to co-regulate and starting to build resilience, adaptability, and collaboration instead of disagreement.

Encouraging co-regulation and self-regulation in teams and individuals forms a feedback loop of emotional safety. This helps both parties approach difference without being trapped by their fear, bias, or judgement. In the short term, this allows for discussion rather than defence. In the long term, it creates increased trust, improved retention, and greater innovation and creativity.

The effect of this on collaboration is transformational. Social psychologist Jonathan Haidt did extensive research into what makes some groups smart and others unintelligent. He found that groups that fixated on a single idea or ideology tended to become closed off to alternative perspectives. This led to illiberal attitudes and impaired collective intelligence.[16] The only cure for this, Haidt said, is consciously creating groups with differing points of view, forcing us to collaborate with people whose opinion is different to our own. This is how we create generative knowledge. Reflective questions like the ones below can help us do this:

- What would you like to achieve by doing X?
- What personal experiences have influenced you to take your position? (This can also be asked during the interview process to invite the person to go deeper into what has shaped and informed them.)
- What is the most important thing you want me to hear and that you would hope I take on board?
- Are you open to hearing a different narrative or thought?

Moving from content to process is also important. Shifting conversations from 'I disagree with you' to 'I notice that we're struggling to hear each other, what's happening here?' helps us stop focusing on what the discussion is about and start paying attention to what's happening for us both. Then, instead of debating who's right, we can step away from the difference and notice how we deal with it.

Navigating difference also requires us to reflect on our positions, particularly our need to persuade or be 'right'. This is why it's so important to spend time noticing our intent, accepting our biases, and checking what drives us to say what we say.

It's also why policies, books, and contracts cannot facilitate navigating difference. While protocol has its place, if we rely on DEI initiatives alone, we will never learn what it *feels* like to safely experience rupture and repair in the relational space. This is the embodiment of these principles as well as their application. Failing to do so prevents us from developing psychological safety and puts us in a state of survival – all because we are still acting out of a state of fear.

Ironically, one of the ways I have found to navigate difference in organisations is to spend time learning about what we share. When we listen to each other's unique experiences of a common event, we allow ourselves to learn about our differences without using labels of 'race', 'gender', 'neurodiversity', or 'religion'. Instead, we focus on what happened, our survival state, and the unique attachment styles we've developed over our lives.

In one organisation, I split the team into pairs and asked them to speak to each other for five uninterrupted minutes on their personal experiences of the Covid lockdown. By the end, each party understood something about the life and inner world of the other as an experience we all in fact shared. This wasn't based on what they *thought* they knew, but on what the other person told them. This is the gateway to empathy, compassion, and curiosity.

PRACTICES TO SUPPORT NAVIGATING DIFFERENCE

The practices of navigating difference are easy to apply. Over time, they can become embedded in your organisation or team and negate the need for complex policies and initiatives.

Here are some ways to navigate difference in day-to-day life:

- Mirroring. Repeating back what the other person has said allows them to hear it again and pause and reflect on whether that's what they meant. It also shows we have heard them and want to understand the intent behind their words. This gives them a corrective, positive felt experience of being heard in the here and now. By mirroring, we also demonstrate presence, helping to regulate the other person's nervous system and reduce defensiveness and the likelihood of entering survival mode. Mirroring can be as simple as asking the other person to confirm what they have said: 'I'm hearing you didn't feel we took on board your ideas. What was that like?' Sometimes this allows the other person to unpack a situation and work out exactly what it is about it that's challenging – this might be something entirely different to what they said the first time round. By mirroring, we give them the opportunity to hear their words back, find the real issue, and go deeper into the conversation we really need to have, and we also give ourselves the reassurance that we've fully understood what is being said.

- Summarising. Helping the other person feel heard regulates their nervous system and invites them to reflect on what's been said. It distils their words into a concise summary, facilitating understanding and allowing the conversation to focus on the one thing that needs to happen *now*. This creates a shared understanding of the conversation, preventing confusion about how we move forward and clarifying the actions we need to follow through. In a one-to-one, summarising can help the other person reflect on the main point of their challenge and work out what their next step should be: 'I can now see that in actual fact there's just one thing you want to discuss, and that's the challenge around resourcing. This seems to be what's causing you and your team the most problems. Is that the key point?'
  'Yes, that's exactly it. Everything else will sort itself out if we focus on resourcing. I think I need to do my homework around what I need and then come back to you.'
  In a team meeting, a leader can use summarising to ensure everyone feels heard: 'Can we just do a whip-round and can everyone share the key thing they are taking from this meeting?' By the facilitator getting everyone to highlight their main takeaway, each person takes ownership for what has happened in the meeting,

knows they are truly 'with' the other people, and understands what matters in the conversation.

- Asking reflective questions. Questions that invite people to share what drives their thinking shift the tone of the conversation from blame and interrogation to reflection and curiosity. Reflective questioning starts within, with asking ourselves to move from 'How can I convince them?' to 'What can I learn from them?' This gives us a get-out from our positions, a way of stepping forward into the space between rather than back behind our shields of difference. You could try asking 'That's a very different way of thinking about the problem. I'm really interested. Can you share more about how you came to that answer?'

Like any of the principles, true navigation of difference requires a commitment. We must be prepared to meet others in the space between and be open to what happens there. This means understanding that our perceptions are limited and influenced by our survival state, our attachment styles, and the narratives we've long held about others and ourselves.

We must also apply and embody the other principles of relational capacity: presence to help us listen, reflection to help us pause and evaluate our reactions and biases, curiosity to open ourselves to learning, respectful candour to allow us to share our perspectives honestly while creating a safe space for others to do the same, and vulnerability to help us embrace the risk of uncertainty.

Navigating difference isn't just about understanding each other. It's about making that understanding count. Without a purpose, even the most relational conversations risk losing their way, as they become an exercise in getting *along* rather than getting *somewhere*.

In the next chapter, we ask: what are we navigating difference for, and how do we go beyond words to reach that goal together?

START WITH THIS

Navigating difference doesn't require a complete cultural overhaul. It can start with a simple shift in how we prepare ourselves to hear and respond – namely, creating the conditions we need to ask curious questions about another's point of view. Try this practice in your next conversation.

The Three-Step Listening Reset:

1. **Pause and notice**
   Before responding, take a moment to notice your reactions. Are you feeling defensive? Are you waiting for your turn to speak rather than truly listening? Simply acknowledging this can help shift the dynamic.
2. **Mirror and summarise**
   Repeat back what the other person said in your own words. Start with 'What I'm hearing you say is…', 'It sounds like you're feeling…' or 'So, if I understand correctly, your concern is…'
3. **Ask a curious question**
   Instead of countering with your own point, ask a question that deepens understanding; for example, 'What's most important to you in this?', 'Can you tell me what about this matters to you?', 'Is there a way we could move this forward in a way that combines our thinking?'

CHAPTER 10

BEING IN SERVICE OF A SHARED GOAL – SERVING OTHERS AND THE COLLECTIVE PURPOSE

"We must be clear at all times about the work we are in service of and maintain an understanding that everything each of us does or says is simply a contribution to our shared endeavour."

WHAT'S IN IT FOR ME?

When Google told thousands of its employees via email they were being laid off, no doubt the effect was devastating. Yet I often wonder what happened for the people left behind. Imagine: one minute you're working for an organisation you love and whose mission and purpose you align with, then that organisation lays off 3,000 of your colleagues overnight. Not only this, but it's done without warning and with no face-to-face communication.

The good news, of course, is that you've kept your job. The bad news is that all the trust, security, and commitment you once felt for your employer is gone. On paper you're a 'survivor'; in reality, you're fighting for your life.

In this scenario, most people would be in survival mode. After all, you're under threat: if 3,000 people can be made redundant without warning, so could you. So the first thought that passes through your mind that day isn't *Phew, I've kept my job*, it's *How do I protect my own interests from now on?*

This is why Google's decision to cut its workforce in this way wasn't just devastating for the people made redundant, but harmful for the business as a whole. Being in survival mode as a result will have changed the relationships of thousands of employees – with both their employer and their colleagues. Instead of asking, *How can I serve this company?*, their question became *What's in this for me?*

Every day, millions of people across the world ask this question. They're performing jobs they're not invested in, jobs that are transactional, functional, and self-serving. They're taking home a pay cheque, but their relationships with their employers and their organisations are limited. They work in quiet competition with their colleagues rather than in connection and collaboration.

This might not seem like a problem. After all, for many people work is simply there to pay the bills. Yet there *is* a problem – and a big one. The relational poverty that results from employees not being in service of something other than themselves doesn't affect just productivity. It affects our mental, emotional, and physical wellbeing, showing up in the form of stress, anxiety, depression, disconnection, and dysregulation, at work and in every aspect of our lives.

It doesn't take a seismic event like redundancy for this to show up. Imagine a CEO who has been instructed by the board to roll out a structural change in a large organisation. Some of the managers are pushing back, as they're concerned about the impact of the restructure on their teams. Frustrated by the resistance, the CEO calls a meeting.

'Look,' he says, 'this restructure is happening whether we like it or not. I understand it's uncomfortable, and I get there will be some pushback. But we need to stop resisting and focus on making it work together. The longer we fight it, the harder it will be.'

It might sound like the CEO is in service of getting things done. After all, he wants to make sure the restructure is rolled out as quickly and painlessly as possible. Yet what if we go beyond the words? What is he really trying to achieve? Is he in service of helping his managers feel at ease? Or of making his job a little easier?

For the managers, their priority is to keep their jobs. They also want to uphold the quality of their work, be fairly rewarded, and feel consulted about key decisions in the process of the restructure.

In a nutshell, they want to feel heard and valued.

So, while both parties are in service of something clear, they're not aligned in their goals. The result is discord. The CEO's words might sound collaborative, but the managers feel patronised and dismissed. They wonder if their parts in the restructure are transactional only, if they're merely cogs in the wheel.

Now imagine a different way. What would have happened if, before he spoke to the team, the CEO had reflected on what they were in service of together? What if he'd been curious about his own agenda, asking himself, *Why Am I Talking?* to assess his immediate need? If he had, he might have realised that what he was actually looking for was compliance: he wanted the managers to shut up, put up, and fall in line so he could get on with the restructure with minimum fuss.

By realising that his own need was having a negative impact on the needs of others, he might have found a better way to handle the restructure.

Let's see a different version of that conversation: 'I can hear this change is unsettling, and I don't expect everyone to be on board right away. My goal isn't to push this through unilaterally but to make sure we have the right conversations about what's working, what's unclear, and what concerns you have. With that in mind, can we talk about what you need to feel confident in this transition?'

Now the managers experience what it's like to be asked about their responses. They feel valued and included, knowing they're partners in the restructure rather than cogs in the wheel. Instead of simply shutting down their resistance, the CEO has showed he's willing to engage with it, letting them know their views are appreciated and respected. The result is that they're more likely to maintain their loyalty to the company and stay in their roles with a commitment to work together, all because the underlying message has changed from *It's my way or the highway* to *I see you. Your concerns matter.*

This gives the managers a corrective felt experience of being heard. On a physical level, their amygdalae – the part of the brain that detects threat – are less activated, helping them to self-regulate more easily. They know they can ask questions, offer insights, and share their vulnerability in a time of uncertainty and change. This psychological safety encourages them to work *with* the restructure rather than against it, because they all have a sense of being in service of the same thing. Instead of a forced directive, the transition becomes a shared goal.

A SUCCESSFUL FAILURE

If you work in an organisation where you're regularly asked to attend awaydays or take part in team-building exercises, you might have experienced the connection and camaraderie of working together to solve a task. You might have also noticed this feeling didn't last. No matter how bonded you felt when building a tower out of spaghetti or capturing a flag in the woods, once you were back in the office, the old ways returned.

Why is the type of teamwork we build so easily out of the office so difficult to recreate when we're back at work?

In 1970, the world watched as the Apollo 13 NASA mission to land on the Moon nearly ended in disaster. Two days after launch, an oxygen tank explosion crippled the spacecraft, forcing the astronauts to abandon the original objective and switch to fighting for survival, with Mission Control on the ground in Houston working tirelessly to find solutions. What I like best about the Apollo 13 story is that the crew's eventual safe return was nicknamed a 'successful failure': while they'd failed to achieve their initial goal, they'd survived disaster against all the odds.

Having a shared endeavour changes the meaning of success. When we're working together towards a specific, named goal, we show up not just as bystanders in the relational space, but as people who have a reason to be there. In other words, we have context. Then we can forget about who's in charge, what's 'in it for me', and whose ego or agenda is most important, and instead focus on what we're doing in the here and now. This is why all those team-building activities give us a sense of bonding: we're focusing on what we're in service of, rather than the story of what's gone before.

Imagine if, in every interaction, meeting, and activity, instead of being led by our own agendas, we knew what we were in service of. Wouldn't that make every conversation easier? We'd be aware of not only what we were saying and the words we used, but *why* we were saying it in the first place. Wouldn't we then find it easier to reflect on our responses? Or be curious about what might be driving others? Wouldn't we feel more able to be vulnerable, admitting what we don't know and where we need help? Wouldn't we be more likely to empathise? To navigate difference? To consider other ways of thinking and working?

When we're in service of our own agendas, even the achievements we label 'success' can feel like failure. Sure, a project might be completed or a deadline might be met, but in achieving this we might have failed completely to meet the individual needs of the team. When we're in service of a shared goal, however, our purpose becomes bigger. We can make a real impact – not because we changed what we did, but because we knew what we were in service of in the first place.

Build a tower. Capture the flag. Bring the astronauts back to Earth. Whatever the mission, when we're in service of a shared goal, we'll always have the opportunity to succeed, because everything each of us says and does is simply a contribution to the team. Then collaboration stops being something we *try* to do and starts to become a description of who we *are* – all because someone began the conversation with a simple question: 'What are we really here to do?'

MORE THAN CLEANERS

Being in service of something other than yourself does not mean sacrificing your needs. In fact, it's a highly pragmatic way to find more meaning in your work. It also reduces anxiety and detachment, takes us out of survival mode, and creates broader, more balanced perspectives.

This doesn't mean we'll never fall into a survival response or repeat the attachment style we learnt in the past. Rather, the felt experience of reflecting on what's happening for us in a particular interaction and on how that impacts what we're trying to achieve as a team allows us to form a new response.

This is not a personality trait, but a choice. In every conversation, project, or organisational scenario we have two options: either we seek the short-term gratification of being right, top, best, or in charge, or we look to the long-term goal of the team.

This demands responsibility. It means reflecting regularly on the consequences of how we show up, acknowledging that the quality of how we relate to other people impacts our interactions today and our future opportunities as a business and a team. In other words, being in service is not a one-time act, but an ongoing mindset: every minute of every day, in every conversation we have, we have the ability to choose.

The results of that choice are huge. In 1998, two university professors, Jane Dutton and Amy Wrzesniewski, asked workers in what they described as menial, low-paid jobs to report their job satisfaction in a survey.[17] One such group was hospital janitors in a major hospital in the US Midwest. In the survey, most of the janitors reported finding their jobs unenjoyable and mundane. However, a subset of the employees – around a third – said they took great satisfaction from their role. When the researchers investigated further, they found these workers held a completely different attitude to the others. While the janitors who didn't enjoy their jobs saw them as a means to an end, the subset of janitors who did find meaning didn't see themselves as janitors at all. Rather, they saw themselves as an integral part of the hospital's professional staff. They might have been performing the same activities as the others and working the same hours, but they'd expanded their understanding of their job description to something more. For them, they were more than cleaners: they were healthcare professionals.

This attitude played out in how the janitors performed their role. Rather than just cleaning, they got to know the patients and their needs. They chose cleaning products that wouldn't irritate them and ensured bed-bound patients had access to fresh drinking water. One janitor reported rearranging pictures on the walls of coma patients to provide a more stimulating environment.

This process of 'job crafting', as the researchers called it, allows workers to find more fulfilment in their work. This means they then look at their roles not as a job to be performed, but as a contribution to the greater purpose of the organisation as a whole. In this case, the janitors didn't see themselves as cleaners, but as contributors to the goal of making people well.

Job crafting doesn't benefit just the individual. A survey by the Temkin Group found that when employees added extra meaning to their work, they were three times more likely to stay late when needed, five times more likely to recommend the company they worked for, and five times more likely to proactively suggest improvements.[18] This phenomenon is also physically measurable: being in service of something greater than ourselves causes stronger cross-network connectivity in the brain. The limbic system, which controls emotion, then works better in partnership with the brain's other systems, increasing brain function and lowering cortisol. This causes us to have lower levels of anxiety and be less likely to overreact to everyday stressors.

Any work, across any industry, can become meaningful when we contribute to a shared goal. And this shift doesn't have to come from the top. In fact, it shouldn't. Job crafting isn't a directive from above but a personal choice, self-created by an individual when they decide to consider their role as a contribution to the whole.

EXCHANGING THE BATON

What led the hospital janitors to choose to add meaning to their role? The answer, as ever, is found not in our actions but in our *interactions*. In other words, the janitors' experiences came not from changing what they *did*, but from changing how they chose to relate to the people around them.

At the 2016 Rio Olympics, the US 4×100m relay team were favourites to win. Yet in the heats, when Allyson Felix tried to pass the baton to sprinter English Gardner, she dropped it. The team was instantly disqualified from the race.

The relay team didn't lose because they were the slowest. In fact, their individual performances were fast. The race was lost in the moment of interaction – the point at which one person's performance touched another's, where the baton was passed from the achievement of one person to the potential achievement of another.

In organisations, as in relay, our interactions shape our outcomes. When we set aside personal agendas and instead work in relationship with the team, pulling together operationally and *relationally*, we not only find meaning in our roles, we create it. We take a decision to do more than simply perform the tasks we are given – we connect in relationship with the people we serve.

This is led by our values. In 2015, a research study by communications consultancy Maitland discovered the top ten core values as stated by member companies of the FTSE 100.[19] They were integrity, respect, innovation, safety, transparency, excellence, teamwork, honesty, trust, and responsibility.

I am fascinated by this report. I wonder why, of all the traits they valued, the majority of organisations put integrity first. Did they want their employees to be morally upright, to hire people who were trustworthy and dependable, people who, in a moral dilemma, would 'do the right thing'? Or did they want to mitigate risk?

When the organisations that chose integrity were asked to clarify their understanding of it, many of them couldn't. It was a trait they sought but couldn't define. I believe so many of them chose integrity because it would mean their people would be a safe pair of hands. They would protect the organisation from harm, never let them down, never show up as a threat. This value didn't come from a place of connection, but a place of fear.

The second thing I notice about this list of values is that many of them are individual. Organisations wanted people who were safe, excellent, responsible, upright. Yet while these values dictate behaviour, they don't ensure connection. They are traits but not relationships; they are focused on what's ethical, rather than what's empathetic.

This is not where true transformation happens. True transformation happens not in us as individuals, but in the space in which we relate to others. Just like in the relay, success isn't about how fast we run, it's about how we pass the baton.

What if, instead of focusing on values that dictate behaviour, organisations chose values based on how we relate to one another? For example, what if, instead of integrity, organisations focused on cultivating self-awareness? Or instead of respect, empathy? Or instead of transparency, effective communication? What if, instead of valuing teamwork, which is surface level, they valued reciprocity? What if, instead of rewarding excellence, they cultivated a culture where everyone understood that the brain is relational?

When we cultivate self-awareness, we get used to reflecting and becoming curious about what happens for us as we interact. This allows us to do more than 'do the right thing' – it allows us to understand how our survival state and attachment styles affect the way we show up in our teams.

When we build empathy, we can truly 'hear' other people, giving us a basis for understanding how others work and how we can most effectively show up with them day to day.

Effective communication means we, as a company, are committed to ensuring we have the one right conversation, instead of the many unhelpful ones that are not in service of our goal. And reciprocity helps us understand that teamwork is about interaction: that when I make myself present, you are more likely to be present; when I am vulnerable, you can be vulnerable, too; when I show curiosity, you're more likely to be curious about me. Not only this, but by me modifying my breathing, heart rhythm, and body language, you're more likely to experience the conversation as a safe place to be.

Finally, when we base our values around the idea that the brain is a relational organ, we start to look at our social experiences in a different way. We reward relationships rather than individual performance, making space for creativity and innovation through our innate desire to find out, connect, and collaborate.

These values are the only ones that can ensure we build teams based on relationships rather than behaviour. Yet in twenty years of working with organisations, I have yet to walk into an office and see them on the wall.

The hospital janitors who found meaning in their work understood how their wellbeing was inextricably connected to others'. They knew true fulfilment comes not from excelling at your job, but from contributing to a collective goal, performing your role only and especially as an integral part of the success of the whole.

When they are relational, organisational values are not abstract. They're pragmatic, concrete, and tangible. We can choose to apply them every minute of every day. We can measure them, support them, even build them into our codes of conduct and reward structures. And when they show up in our interactions regularly, they affect our relationships, which in turn dictate our wellness and the organisational health of the business as a whole.

Instead of asking how your employees are performing against your company values, ask them this: 'What type of conversations are you having within your team? Where? In the hallways? Via email and web chats? With your superiors, colleagues, clients, and suppliers? Are these conversations reflective and curious – ones where you are vulnerable, honest, and empathic, genuinely seeking to understand what's happening for you, the other, and in the space between? Or are you so stuck in your own survival mode and attachment styles that you cannot even hear what the other is saying? Worse, are you refusing to step into that space at all because you're in service only of mitigating the risk to you and your organisation in the short term?'

An interesting point I've noticed is that, when organisations focus on self-awareness, empathy, effective communication, reciprocity, and the brain's innate desire to relate to others, values like integrity, excellence, and trust tend to slide into place. This is because when we believe that the brain is relational, we naturally build trust because we're operating 'in the space' rather than in our own isolated ways. When we have reciprocity, we naturally allow for teamwork and innovation because everything we do is given and received in equal measure. We also end up 'doing the right thing' and taking responsibility, because we understand the impact of our actions on others.

Likewise, where we have empathy, we have respect; where we have effective communication, we have transparency; where we have self-awareness, we naturally create the conditions to excel.

If we want to build organisations that truly thrive, we need to go beyond the traits of the individual. We need instead to pay attention to what happens in the space between, and when we do, we need to ask a different question. Instead of *What's in this for me?*, we ask ourselves, *How can I help?*

BUILDING BEING IN SERVICE IN ORGANISATIONS

While applying and embodying the principles and practices in this book will improve the quality of your conversations, facilitating these in organisations starts with a deeper question: what's driving your communication in the first place?

Every conversation has an unspoken driver. When leaders aren't conscious of what they're in service of, they often default to control, defensiveness, or self-preservation. But when they step back and set a clear intention, they create conversations that build trust, alignment, and change. Remember: your leadership capacity is only as strong as your ability to hold expansive conversations. By asking 'How can I help?', we can become not just problem solvers but space holders – in other words, the people who facilitate finding the answer in ways that are not bound by the obvious.

When we lead with intention, we realise that our role is not to *dictate* solutions but to create the space where the best solutions emerge. This means leaving our preconceptions about what the answer is at the door and sitting in uncertainty. Counter-intuitively, this is efficient rather than inefficient leadership: the best communication isn't talking less, but having one conversation and the right conversation.

When we learn to speak 'in service of' – and when what we are in service of is alignment, possibility, and connection – conversations open up in new ways. Here are three examples:

- 'How do I get my team on board?' becomes 'What are we trying to create together?'
- 'How do I get them to listen?' becomes 'What needs to be heard?'
- 'How do I avoid resistance?' becomes 'What is this resistance telling me?'

This is the beginning of shifting from 'me' to 'we' – moving from individual-driven transmission to collective-driven communication. This requires an intentional move away from personal agenda, defensiveness, and transactional exchanges, and towards shared purpose, mutual accountability, and curiosity.

This means starting every conversation with a shared intention. Before diving into problem-solving, ask:

- What are we here to create together in this conversation?
- What do we need this discussion to serve?
- What would success look like for all of us, not just as individuals?

It also means replacing the notion of 'Who's right?' with 'What's missing?' Where disagreements exist, instead of defending personal viewpoints, ask if there are any perspectives that haven't yet been considered. How could ideas build on each other instead of competing?

This moves conversations from being ego-driven to collaborative processes of problem-solving.

PRACTICES TO SUPPORT BEING IN SERVICE

For teams to be truly in service of a shared goal, we must be able to clarify what is happening and have accountability on commitments. Here are some more ways to cultivate being in service in day-to-day life:

- Practise accountability. Without explicitly defined expectations, even the most well-intentioned teams risk misalignment, ambiguity, and inefficiency. When accountability is framed not as blame and shame, but as a commitment to collective success, it becomes a driver of trust and ownership, rather than a weapon. This means defining commitments with precision. Intentions like 'Let's improve communication' or 'We should collaborate more' allow misinterpretation and inconsistency. Commitments should be:
    - Specific, measurable, and time-bound. For example, 'We'll provide project updates every Friday' or 'We'll respond to client emails within twenty-four hours.'
    - Co-created rather than imposed. People are more likely to follow through when they have a say in what they're accountable for.
    - Free of blame. Check-ins should focus on progress, not policing – ask 'What's helping us stay on track?' rather than 'Who's not delivering?'
    - Driven by curiosity rather than criticism. Move from 'Why haven't you done this?' to 'What might you need to meet this commitment?'

- Use 'we' language. Small language shifts make a big difference. For example:
  - 'That's not my responsibility' becomes 'How can we solve this together?'
  - 'Here's my take' becomes 'What's the best path forward for us as a team?'
- Clarify. By checking in before moving on, we can limit the use of assumption and identify what we are in service of, without having the same conversations over and over. Instead of assuming intent, develop the habit of asking:
  - 'Before we move forward, can we all agree on what success looks like here?'
  - I'm hearing you say X. Is that what you mean?'

This aligns expectations so that decisions actually stick. We can seek further interpretation by asking:

- 'Can you expand on what you mean by that?'
- 'It sounds like you're saying X – is that correct?'

This prevents misinterpretation and builds trust, ensuring everyone feels heard. Clarifying isn't just about repeating back what someone said – it's making sure every conversation serves the right purpose. It's the bridge between intention and impact, ensuring what's being communicated aligns with what needs to be discussed. By clarifying, we slow the conversation down and make sure we're not reacting to a misunderstanding. This keeps the focus on what needs to be addressed rather than the surface-level issues. In other words, clarifying helps shift from *content* to *process*, ensuring we're having one conversation and the right conversation.

It also creates space for more honest dialogue. People often voice half-formed thoughts, especially in high-stakes conversations. Clarifying signals that *I'm here to understand, not just respond.* This encourages team members to say what they mean instead of defaulting to what they think is safe. In doing this, we shift the energy from defensiveness to curiosity.

In 2022, after the Covid pandemic, Maitland repeated its values survey. I found the results fascinating. Integrity was no longer the most common value in organisations – it had been replaced by another: collaboration.

When I wonder what might have caused this shift, I remember that, in those seven years since the original survey, the world had changed. From the start of 2020, businesses had a bigger problem to solve than their individual purposes: the response to the Covid pandemic. I wonder if they realised that the way we work depends not on the individual, but on what we are committed to achieve as a group. The examples of being in service in this way are many: some of the biggest names in UK manufacturing joined together with Formula 1 teams to produce ten years' supply of ventilators in the space of ten weeks; Oxford University's Jenner Institute partnered with pharmaceutical giant AstraZeneca to produce a vaccine in less than a year; NHS departments shared staff to deploy resources where they were most needed.

When we have a shared endeavour – whether it's responding to a global pandemic or simply working together to solve a thorny problem – we realise the power of being in service of a wider goal. We understand not only that our interactions determine our outcomes, but that our values determine the quality of those interactions. Our ability to be self-aware, to empathise, to communicate effectively, to reciprocate, and to understand that we are relational by nature allows us to take the role we've been given and apply ourselves for the good of the whole.

This shift – from personal performance to reciprocal relationships – is made possible only by applying and embodying the principles we have covered so far in this book: presence, reflection, curiosity, respectful candour, vulnerability, and navigating difference. It's the gulf between an organisation with a 'mission' and an organisation with employees who are truly in service, because while the former is a collection of words that identify a goal, the latter is beyond words – a felt experience in the space between.

START WITH THIS

Before your next conversation or meeting, pause for ten seconds and ask yourself:

- What am I in service of in this conversation?
- Am I here to control, convince, or contribute?
- How can I create space for shared insight instead of driving my own agenda?

During the conversation, notice when you're about to interrupt, dismiss an idea, or push your own opinion. Instead of reacting, take a breath and ask:

- What's missing?' (Rather than 'Who's right?')
- What's needed here?' (Rather than 'What do I want to say next?')

After the conversation, take thirty seconds to reflect by asking yourself:

- Did I help create alignment and clarity?
- Did I listen to understand, or just to respond?
- How could I shift my approach next time to be in greater service of the shared goal?

CHAPTER 11

A MINDSET OF ABUNDANCE – BELIEVING IN SHARED PROSPERITY

"Everything – whether consciously constructive or not – moves us forward and upward."

REWILDING

In her book *Wilding*, Isabella Tree describes how she and her husband, Charlie Burrell, decided to stop farming their 3,500-acre farm in West Sussex and let nature take over. For years, the farm's clay-heavy soil had been poorly suited for intensive arable farming. Pesticides and fertilisers had also depleted the soil, causing erosion and reducing biodiversity. Intensive farming methods weren't just harming the farm's long-term yields; they were destroying its ecosystem. Eventually, the farm was at a point where it was barely breaking even. The Burrells needed a leap of faith.

The Burrells stopped cultivating the land. They introduced native, free-roaming grazing animals, such as Tamworth pigs, Exmoor ponies, and longhorn cattle. Then they reconnected the waterways, replacing the artificial channels and canals that had been constructed to irrigate the farm. They allowed wild plants and shrubs to take over. Bit by bit, they moved away from managing the farm and started to act as its facilitators.

Far from the farm becoming a chaotic and overgrown wilderness, the Burrells found it began to **self-organise**. Without chemical pesticides, wildflowers and grasses returned, attracting insects and insect-eating birds, bats, and other creatures. Within a few years, rare species such as turtle doves, nightingales, peregrine falcons, and lesser-spotted woodpeckers began to colonise. A decade later, the Burrells' degraded agricultural land has become a functioning ecosystem, abundant with life.

In organisations, 'abundance' often means 'more': more money, more people, more productivity, more efficiency, more technology, more time. We believe the greater the input, the greater the output – in other words, the better the resources we have, the better the results we'll get.

You might have thought along these lines yourself: *If only I had more time, I could be a better leader. We need more policies in place to reduce conflict and improve communication. A new online system would help us reduce inefficiencies. There aren't enough hours in the day to be the business we want to be.*

Is this true? Are organisations held back by a lack of 'stuff'? Or are we focusing on a scarcity of resource when really we have a scarcity of belief?

Whether it's cracks forming in a growing organisation, missed deadlines, micromanagement, office politics, disengagement, generational or gender divides, or artificially 'collaborative' cultures, the root cause is the same. In seeking *more*, we fail to realise that what we need is already there. We simply need to believe in what's possible when we go back to the truth of who we are.

When I work with organisations and individuals who are in survival mode, I see how people and teams can easily become prisoners to their attachment styles. This leads to them becoming dysregulated in their responses, subject to their preconceived assumptions and biases, unproductive, polluted, and reduced. Their environment has been so intensively 'managed', it's as depleted as the soil on the Burrells' farm. By spending so much time trying to manage and control, they've failed to notice our innate and abundant ability to relate to other people.

When we approach organisations and teams with the idea that the brain is a relational organ, we realise that everything we need to build a successful organisation is already there. Not only this, we also have the capacity to create it every day – in every interaction, every meeting, every conversation, and every decision. To create the abundance we seek in our teams and organisations, we don't need more resources, we simply need space and belief. This means replacing control with connection, protocol with principles, and policy with possibility so we can allow people to work together in their ecosystem, in relationship with each other and in service of a shared goal. Then we realise that collaboration and relationship are not only possible, but probable.

This requires us to show up in the space between, to reflect on our responses, to get curious about others, and to be vulnerable, honest, and available to truly hear what's happening for us all. Only then does our ability to coexist become clear, allowing us to step away from our need to control, maximise, manipulate, and profit, and instead learn to collaborate in a self-organising way. We then realise that abundance doesn't start with what we *have*, but with what we believe is possible through our connection with others. When we create space for this connection, we realise that there isn't a challenge, problem, or conversation we can't face.

BEYOND OPTIMISM

The term 'abundance mindset' was first coined by Stephen R. Covey in 1989, in his bestselling book *The 7 Habits of Highly Effective People*. According to Covey, those choosing an abundance mindset believe there are unlimited resources available for every individual and that long-term success warrants the creation of a win-win situation for all.

When we hold a mindset of abundance, we give ourselves the opportunity to navigate our way through discord. Instead of seeing it as a problem, we see it as an opportunity for growth. We then make better decisions and choices, as we aren't coming from a place of fear and survival, but are leaning into what is here, in the present, right now. We're then more likely to celebrate others' successes, more likely to be present, and more likely to be reciprocal in our relationships.

The benefits of this for the individual are clear: we're less anxious, more engaged, more positive, more fulfilled. For teams and organisations, however, it changes everything. When we embrace this mindset as a group, we're more inclined to share resources and we have better ideas and more collective energy because we not only believe the answers are available, we know there's enough success to go round. This generosity creates a collaborative environment where challenges are seen as opportunities for innovation and harnessing collective strengths, not roadblocks of discord and disagreement.

When we stop fighting for survival and start allowing what's naturally present to self-organise into a thriving ecosystem, we start to see a different way. We believe in what's possible, and, as a result of this belief, we have the courage to step into our ability to connect. Instead of asking 'What needs to be fixed?', we ask 'What would be possible if we could create an environment where every voice feels safe to be heard?'

This is not positive thinking or optimism, but a pragmatic approach that combines curiosity and hope to find real and unthought-of opportunities. I've seen first-hand the destruction caused by 'false positivity' – when organisations forge ahead with a particular path when it's clear the approach won't bring results. By refusing to see anything other than the positive, disallowing dissent, and discouraging criticism and negative feedback, we can miss what genuinely needs our attention. That might be our own behaviour, the product, the team, the organisation, or even the relational space itself. False positivity stops us revealing vulnerabilities, stifles critical thinking and respectful candour, and prevents us from moving forward with solutions in service of what we need to achieve. It stops us asking 'What conversations aren't people having because they don't believe they can?'

A senior creative I worked with demonstrated this perfectly when he told me how he didn't feel a current project was of a high enough standard for a high-profile customer. We'll call him Michael.

'I feel like we're under-delivering on what we promised,' he said. 'No one else seems to think it's an issue, but it's just not the quality I'm used to.'

I decided to ask a question. 'From what I'm hearing, it sounds like you feel quite strongly about this. Were you able to share your thinking with the project manager?'

He laughed. 'Are you crazy? All she wants to hear is that everything's on time. She doesn't want to hear any negative talk, or that there's something that might need fixing. I tried to raise it once and she just said, "The team's doing a great job, Michael. Don't rock the boat."'

As a result of this false optimism, Michael had no psychological safety to engage in vulnerability or respectful candour. The lack of a mindset of abundance – not 'this is perfect' but 'we can make it better' – meant he didn't feel able to raise the problem. As a result, the team couldn't lean into the discomfort of the project not being quite right and couldn't be curious about a higher-quality solution. They'd also never increase their creativity and innovation, because the project manager didn't have faith in the team's ability to do so.

Positive thinking like this often becomes an either/or position: *either* we are positive *or* we are negative. Yet the reality in organisations is more nuanced – after all, challenge can exist alongside possibility. A mindset of abundance is more about the 'and': 'I can really hear your pride in the team's work *and* that you feel the project needs a rethink. What's the one thing you need most to take this to the next level?'

This form of questioning not only invites reflection but engages curiosity, so the person can find the answer themselves and also be vulnerable enough to reveal what's getting in the way. This both encourages and requires a mindset of abundance about what's possible – even in terms of our own responses. When we reflect on our survival state or attachment style and understand how it developed – in other words, 'think about our thinking' – we can work on regulating our emotions. Having confidence in our ability to do this takes us out of a scarcity mindset and into more abundant thinking. Then, instead of activating the brain's stress response, releasing 'survival' hormones like cortisol and causing tunnel vision, we engage both the prefrontal cortex and the anterior cingulate cortex. This is the region of the brain that's associated with forward-focused behaviour, empathy, adaptability, and resilience. When we perceive abundance, instead of cortisol we release dopamine and other neurotransmitters, giving us feelings of hope and creativity that allow us to explore possibilities and come up with innovative solutions.

In this way, having a mindset of abundance gives us the willingness to see what we have in the here and now, as well as the hope and belief we can have more. We then know we will not only be able to solve the challenges with which we're faced, but also, in the process of that work, feel seen, known, heard, and valued, giving us the felt experience that we are contributing to the team and finding purpose in what we do.

These challenges are not always easy, and this is where a mindset of abundance truly helps us be relational. It is precisely in the difficult times, when we are perhaps faced with hard decisions, when we need to remember what's possible when we show up effectively in the space between.

A DIFFERENT TYPE OF GRATITUDE

It's scientifically understood that practising gratitude improves mental health, lifts mood, and contributes to overall wellbeing and self-esteem.[20] Yet gratitude, when practised authentically, goes far beyond being an individual emotion or activity. When adopted as a mindset, it fundamentally changes how we relate to others and in the space between us.

Expressing gratitude creates an upward spiral of positive emotion. It can be as simple as showing appreciation for a moment of connection: 'Thanks for really hearing me, it helps so much.' This signals acknowledgement and appreciation to the other, which in turn invites them to be open and trust because they believe in the power of relationship when they do. It also inspires action. When we feel grateful, we're more likely to give back or 'pay it forward' – changing our behaviour and presence because we see the effectiveness of what that does in others. This is the beginning of true transformation in organisations.

Far from being an exercise in journaling or list-making, gratitude is a mindset that's adopted cognitively, physiologically, and emotionally – in other words, it is both applied *and* embodied as a felt experience in our systems. Cognitively, it shifts our focus from scarcity ('What's missing?') to abundance ('What can we do in the here and now?'). Emotionally, it creates connection and reciprocity, allowing us to come out of survival state in order to co-regulate and connect. And physiologically, gratitude activates the parasympathetic nervous system, calming the body and reducing stress. This allows us to be more open and less defensive in our interactions.

For this reason, gratitude is not just an internal process. In fact, it's not enough to *feel* grateful at all. The emotion must manifest in how we interact. This helps us build a more truthful representation of ourselves, the other, and the relational space, reducing the amount of time we spend ruminating in pessimistic, restrictive thought patterns, and helping us stay grounded enough to accept the present situation. Then, even in a challenging scenario, we can support co-regulation and feel seen, heard, and understood.

BUILDING A MINDSET OF ABUNDANCE IN ORGANISATIONS

All of the other principles in this book rely on a mindset of abundance. Yet, incredibly, they also create it. When we have a mindset of abundance, we are more likely to be present, because rather than acting out of fear or survival, we can see the bigger picture in the here and now. It also invites us to reflect, making us open to exploring meaning and working on our self-regulation. Then we can move beyond survival and into a place of possibility and opportunity.

Curiosity also facilitates a mindset of abundance, and, at the same time, that abundant thinking allows us to be curious. When we're in survival mode we reinforce a 'me versus you', 'right versus wrong', 'good versus bad' position. This makes collaborating difficult, because we're always afraid to try something new, hear a different viewpoint, or do something in a way we haven't tried before. With an abundant mindset, however, we're more likely to ask about possible solutions, more open to testing innovation, and more tolerant of new approaches, opinions, and points of view.

An abundant mindset inspires radical candour. It allows us to paint a picture of what's possible – without blaming and shaming – to facilitate growth. When we enter a conversation with dread rather than abundance, it's impossible to engage in respectful candour in a way that allows both parties to hear, because we're restricted by the lack of psychological safety in that space. When we engage in respectful candour in a mindset of abundance, however, we can be both relational and direct. We can be empathic at the same time as challenging, caring at the same time as focused, both grateful for their support and keen to ask for something different because we believe in the possibility of what we can do.

Navigating difference is also expedited by a mindset of abundance. When we believe in a world where the pie is only so big, it's much more difficult to work with diverse approaches, because our attitude of deficit says, *If you get something, I lose something.* A mindset of abundance, however, allows us to have not only differences in thinking but the belief that those differences will enrich our lives, our products, our teams, our organisations, our relationships, and the space between us. In other words, there isn't a limit to how much pie we can make.

When we have a mindset of abundance, we can be vulnerable. We can ride the wave of emotions and not get stuck in them, because we understand we have the resilience both individually and collectively to 'be' with what we are experiencing. We then know we are not alone in what we are experiencing, because, while the emotion is ours alone, we can co-regulate in the space between by knowing the other is there for us. This doesn't mean a team that colludes or enables the survival state and attachment styles, but one where its members know they can get through this together.

When we're in service of a shared goal, we're also more likely to have a mindset of abundance. We're more willing to ask how we can help, because we believe we can find the right resources together. We can then put ourselves last because we're willing to think together about what we can do for the good of the team.

Having a mindset of abundance means not being afraid to ask the right questions, not shying away from feedback, and not avoiding vulnerability, because we know we can successfully navigate whatever comes up in service of our shared experience. Communicating this assurance to the other in the space between doesn't let them know just what's possible. It lets them know they're in a relationship that's safe.

One way of doing this is through validation. When we listen to someone's experience only waiting to respond, or to tell them what to do, to give advice, or to share a story about ourselves, we immediately invalidate what's happening for them with responses like 'Oh, that's nothing, you should hear what happened to me', 'You'll be fine', 'Don't worry it will get easier' and 'I'm sure they didn't mean to do that to you.'

Witnessing and giving someone space to have their experience, on the other hand, helps that person feel heard and understood. Research shows that verbal validation calms us physically and is an effective way to co-regulate, helping us to notice an experience and then move past it.

We don't have to rely on others to do this – we can offer it to ourselves. To truly validate, however, we must be comfortable with a wide range of emotions – including our sense of helplessness, powerlessness, uncertainty, resentment, disappointment, frustration, confusion, or fear. We must also be comfortable with more positive emotions, such as joy, excitement, and enthusiasm. True validation allows for *any* emotion to be in the space and gives the person permission to safely engage with it before moving on.

Needless to say, to validate we need to be able to hear. This means we need to be regulated and not in a survival state or acting out our own attachment styles. Validation is powerful precisely because it slows the conversation down, allowing us to move away from the *content* of what's being said and to pay attention to the *process*. It also allows the other to begin to connect with the felt experience of being heard and seen. This often helps a person to go beyond the 'story' to their underlying need. By validating that need, we show them what they're in service of even before they speak.

Here are some examples of validating:

- 'Given what you have shared about X, it makes sense to me that you feel that way.'
- 'I really hear how hard you have found working with X on that project.'
- 'I hear you.'
- 'Gosh, that sounds really tough.'
- That's fantastic. It sounds like you really overcame a massive challenge there and are very happy with the outcome. How did you do that?'

As this language shows, to validate we have to 'hear' the other at a deeper level – beyond our defences, beyond right and wrong, beyond you versus me, beyond good versus bad – simply being present, with the person, in their experience.

Whether we use 'limiting' language or 'affirming' language can show us if someone has a mindset of abundance. When we use directives ('Stop' or 'Don't') or absolutes ('Always' or 'Never') we limit the conversation to preconceived biases and assumptions. For example:

- 'Stop worrying, you'll be fine.'
- 'Well, that was an epic fail.'
- 'Sarah never shows up on time.'
- 'Mark always gets it wrong.'
- 'Just smile.'

When we switch this to affirming language, however, we open up possibilities for problem-solving, understanding and connection:

- 'Stop worrying, you'll be fine' becomes 'I can hear this is challenging for you. What's the one thing you need right now?'
- 'Well, that was an epic fail' becomes 'I really get that didn't go to plan. What would you want to do differently next time?'
- 'Sarah never shows up on time' becomes 'I notice Sarah struggles to show up on time. I wonder what's happening for her?'
- 'Mark always gets it wrong' becomes 'I'm noticing Mark's made a couple of mistakes recently. I think I should go and chat to him and find out what's happening for him.'
- 'Just smile' becomes 'I can see you're feeling rather anxious about this. Would it be OK if we took a moment to talk it through?'

This kind of language shows the other that we are willing to step into the space between and that we believe in our ability to facilitate what needs to happen. This helps them also to show up, co-regulate, and be willing to look for the most effective and appropriate way forward. This is essential if we are to create good mental health and wellbeing at work.

PRACTICES TO SUPPORT A MINDSET OF ABUNDANCE

Here are some simple ways to invite your whole being to move towards integrating a mindset of abundance:

- Build a relational 'bank' for you and others through words that reflect gratitude. Examples could be 'Thank you for working with me on this project, I've really appreciated you bringing a different perspective' or 'Thanks for sharing that. I hadn't thought about it that way before' or 'I really enjoyed our conversation.'
- Show a mindset of abundance through your actions. Invite your employees to tell you more about their thinking around a particular idea or project; send them on a course to improve their skills; offer to mentor them; ask the most junior member of staff to lead the next team meeting.
- When you have a challenge you've been sitting with for a while and have no answer to, try asking people unrelated to the task for their thinking. What do they think might be getting in the way of solving this problem?
- Offer your team time to work on other projects. These might have nothing to do with work. Trust in their ability to use that space to generate ideas on how to solve issues within the organisation, too.

When Isabella Tree and Charlie Burrell rewilded their farm, the result was transformational. To achieve this, they had to envisage a different world to the one they knew. When Isabella writes about the depletion of the intensively farmed soil, I can't help thinking she could just as easily have been writing about organisations:

> *Over the years modern farming has reduced soil to 'dirt' – a sterile medium in which plants struggle to grow without artificial fertilisers. It is a self-perpetuating cycle of destruction and chemical dependence...*

This relational poverty – the result of which we see in our teams' disconnection, disengagement, dysregulation, and discord – is not the way humans were meant to be. The neuroplasticity of our brains has meant we have been vulnerable – to the dynamics of our relationships and the ruptures we so inevitably experience as part of human life.

Yet there is a different way. As Isabella writes:

> *We forget, in a world completely transformed by man, that what we're looking at is not necessarily the environment wildlife prefer, but the depleted remnant that wildlife is having to cope with.*

Transforming our organisations from sterile, depleted environments where people struggle to thrive into abundant, messy, self-organising spaces where we effectively coexist requires us to awaken our faith. We must imagine a world where how we were meant to be is how we are. Rewilding the farm might have been messier, but it wasn't chaotic. Neither are relational organisations. Each species, while it has its own needs, tendencies, and adaptations, learns in time to work in harmony with the others. Ruptures, while frequent, are short-lived and easily repaired. Each entity works together with the next because it knows its own actions help what the others do, too. In this sense, each way of working, each thought, each approach enables the other to exist as well – together, openly, and in service of what we're all trying to achieve.

Having a mindset of abundance is about believing and embodying the belief that we can step into the space between us – even when it's messy. I want to leave you with a story I read about some children at a primary school who were asked to write what love meant for them. Most of the children wrote about a parent, a grandparent, or even a pet or friend. One six-year-old girl, however, wrote this:

> *Love is when you're missing some of your teeth. But you're not afraid to smile because you know your friends still love you, even though some of you is missing.*

A mindset of abundance is not about perfection. It means not being afraid to smile. It's saying 'Here I am, in my human imperfection, but I trust you will accept that and work with me anyway – not because I am perfect but because I am a human. Just like you.'

When I am curious, reflective, and respectfully candid, when I ask what is happening for you and share what is happening for me, when I let you see my vulnerability, when I ask you how what we are doing is in service of the goal we share, I can believe we will find a way together. That's what a mindset of abundance is: knowing I will be accepted, loved, and heard and that there's no conversation we can't have, because we know the *process* of what we're going to say is more powerful than the words.

For too long we have focused on the wellbeing of individuals, forgetting that we are relational beings designed to live in a network of connection with others. When we have belief in our ability to do this, we create an environment that's more than a collection of individuals.

It's an ecosystem.

START WITH THIS

The next time you have an interaction or conversation, think about the process of that conversation as an opportunity for connection by trying the following:

- Regulate yourself.
- Identify the other person's emotion – not by making it up, but because you heard them say it.
- Clarify this with them: 'From what you're sharing I'm hearing that you feel quite disappointed. That's my word for it – what would yours be?'
- Validate the emotion.
- Seek to understand what's driving that emotion and take time to be with someone while they unpack something: 'I can really hear how frustrated you are and I'd really like to understand what's driving that frustration. Can you tell me more?'

When we are truly interested in the other – not to defend, be right, or even to agree, but to truly hear and understand them – we embody a mindset of abundance. We are effectively saying 'It's OK, I trust that we can do this, even if you're struggling right now. I believe in you and your ability to work this out.'

CHAPTER 12

PUTTING IT INTO PRACTICE

In this chapter, I want to bring to life how conversations – when approached relationally – can, rather than representing what's wrong in organisations, be a powerful force for good.

Many of the books you might have read about communication at work will focus on methods, tips, and tricks. As you will by now know, this book focuses instead on the application of relational principles. These take into account that while relating is a messy, complex business, it is also wonderfully self-organising. The following real-life conversations show how that is possible. As well as how to apply these principles, they show how we can embody them – in other words, how we can experience the effect of these principles at an autonomic, physiological level. Before I share the conversations, let me show you what this means.

When a person enters a conversation and the other person is in survival mode – dysregulated, mitigating risk, defensive, and afraid – it is impossible for them to hear what the other is saying. If, however, they come to the conversation regulated, present, reflective, and curious, prepared to be vulnerable and apply all the other principles in this book, something happens not just to them, but to the other. Even if the other has come to that interaction in a dysregulated way, the application of the principles causes something to shift.

First, when the speaker shows they are present, the other person gets a physical experience of what it's like to be heard. Their system calms. They receive eye contact. Their whole body recognises that here is someone available and attuned to hear them out – not only to listen but to understand them on a deeper level.

When the speaker then pauses to reflect – for example, by asking 'What's happening for you?' – the other experiences what it's like to connect with a response. They might notice their own sense of anxiety, or defensiveness, or simply their impatience to return to what they were doing. Rather than putting these emotions in charge of the conversation, they can instead make meaning from them, because the other has given the time to do so.

Next, if the speaker shows curiosity – for example, by being willing to hear a different point of view rather than relying on their own bias – the other feels what it's like to be noticed. This further calms their system, showing them this is a space where their answers will be taken into account rather than assumed or dismissed. The emotional regulation this allows changes the conversation completely. From now on, it's a space where two people can come outside survival mode and instead interact on a level that allows them to relate to each other. This not only changes what is said, it changes their entire experience.

I cannot overstate the power of this process in organisations and teams. Whether we like it or not (and whether we know it or not), each of us brings to work a set of behaviours, responses, beliefs, and stories. These have resulted from the way we've experienced people in the past – either recently or years ago when we were children. These attachment styles – whether anxious, avoidant, or disorganised – will *always* show up in our interactions and physiological responses. Remember: our past votes loudly in our present.

Our only hope of having powerful, connective relationships that encourage collaboration, trust, psychological safety, and respect is to experience those interactions in a different way. In fact, change can happen *only* when we have a positive, corrective felt experience in the here and now.

When we do, it changes everything.

You might not think these changes can happen overnight, and, of course, you'd be right. However, they can happen remarkably quickly. In fact, sometimes it takes only one positive, corrective felt experience in a conversation, right here, right now, for the system to start to repair. Suddenly, the stories from the past (*No one ever listens to me, My work isn't valued, I'm out of my depth, I have to fight to survive*) don't seem so true. We realise that our narratives are just that – our narratives.

Instead, we experience a different way: someone listening to truly hear, someone who is curious about my thoughts, someone prepared to hear my point of view. The sensations this causes in the body are lightning fast. It's why I believe in the power of these principles not just in the long term, but in the very next interaction you have. That's what I hope to show you here.

There is something else to remember. In every conversation there is not just you and me, but a third entity: the space between.

So, what happens there when two people relate to each other?

Just as presence, reflection, curiosity, respectful candour, vulnerability, navigating difference, being in service of a shared goal, and a mindset of abundance create a positive, corrective experience in you and me, they also have a transformative effect on the relational space.

The space becomes somewhere safe. It becomes the field, in Rumi's famous poem, beyond right and wrong, where we can meet. It's where we can put aside ego, 'getting ahead', company politics, even organisational hierarchies, and instead meet as two humans with relational brains wired to connect. When we do so, the space itself is changed – not just between us, but between the people in the organisation as a whole.

In the following two exchanges, I want to show you how this is possible. In each, you can see the principles in this book at work. You can also see the importance of process over content – that the subject of the conversations is not as important as what is happening behind the scenes: the transformative, wonderful power of relationship that goes beyond words.

These are not scripts. I don't encourage conversations to be thought out in advance, transactional, or to follow protocol. Instead, I want to show you how a conversation can evolve with meaning and connection when two people embody and apply the principles in this book in an authentic, self-organising way. This will show you they are not abstract ideals but rather practical, dynamic ways of being in conversation. They allow us to engage with others at a level that's both human and impactful, helping us to gain clarity about ourselves, our motivations, and our readiness for change. At the same time, they can transform organisations at the highest level: in hiring, in HR management, in conflict resolution, in innovation, in team dynamics, and in strategy.

AN INTERVIEW TURNING POINT

At the request of a CEO, I was asked to meet with a potential candidate – let's call him Jim – to interview him for a senior role. Jim had been introduced to the company through a contact, and while he had showed genuine interest in the business, he had also indicated that he was unsure whether he wanted to re-enter the corporate world after taking some time out for his mental health.

The CEO asked me to assess two things: was Jim truly ready to return to corporate life? And, if so, why this company, and why now?

From the outset, I knew I wanted to focus on being present – fully attuned and aligned with Jim in the here and now.

This would help me not only truly hear what Jim was saying, but have the time to pause and reflect on his and my responses.

After introductions, I asked one simple, open-ended question: 'I'm really curious about your experience of the conversations you've been having with the CEO. Can you tell me more about that?'

Jim paused – then launched into a detailed fifteen-minute monologue about the business, the market, and the product. While the content was informative, what truly caught my attention was his consistent use of the word 'we' when referencing the business: 'What we need to do is...'

This subtle choice of language became a turning point for the conversation.

Rather than proceeding with standard questions about his career, experience, or interest in the role, I decided to tune into Jim's language and reflect on what it might mean. I asked, 'I notice you use the word "we" whenever you mention something to be considered about the business. Is that something you've noticed too?'

Jim paused, suddenly becoming genuinely reflective. 'I really hadn't noticed. How interesting.'

My willingness to be respectfully candid – in this case, through a gentle observation – opened the door to a deeper inquiry. I followed up with: 'What do you make of that?'

'Well, there's clearly something about this role and the business that's exciting me. Which is interesting, because until this moment, I would have said the idea of going back into the industry left me feeling nauseous.'

I asked, 'Is this something we can explore a little more?' He agreed.

Jim had spoken previously about taking time out from work due to burnout. I asked him to estimate how much of him still felt burnt out versus how much felt curious or excited about the role. He said, 'At first, I was definitely 95%

burnt out and only 5% curious. Now I'd say I'm 65% curious and 35% burnt out.'

'What do you think has shifted the balance?'

Jim reflected again and replied, 'There's no pressure. I'm seeing this as a project, not a job.'

I probed further: 'And what does seeing it as a project do to the nausea you talked about earlier?'

He smiled. 'It's gone.'

Our mutual vulnerability – Jim's willingness to explore unexpected emotions and my openness to follow the unknown – helped him see how his experience of himself was shifting in the here and now. We were also being curious about each other, as neither of us had anticipated the direction the conversation took.

Throughout the conversation, I held a mindset of abundance: we didn't need to force a decision or rush to an outcome here; we were merely exploring responses. There was space between us to do this: to reflect and allow clarity to emerge. My focus wasn't on the functional aspects of Jim's career or the company's needs, but on being in service of a shared goal: understanding if this was the right fit for Jim and the organisation.

Instead of fixating on what Jim could offer the business right now, it was more important for us to attend to *what was happening in the moment*: his language, his shifting emotions, and his bodily sensations (for example, the nausea). That shift from content to process enabled Jim to connect more consciously to his relationship with burnout and his interest in the company.

I had one last question for Jim: 'How much of the shift in your percentages is because you're thinking about this role as a project, not a job?'

'Definitely because I see it as a project. If I thought of it as a job, I think the nausea would be back.'

This conversation helped Jim realise two important things:

1. His subconscious was more invested than he had initially believed.
2. He wasn't ready for a full-time corporate role, but the *project* nature of the work was energising.

For me, it became clear that Jim's interest was genuine but contingent on framing the work as a project. I gained valuable insight into what would re-engage him – the freedom to explore without pressure – and also into his evolving relationship with his own mental wellness.

For the CEO, this meant a transformational approach to recruitment. Instead of pushing for a hire, he decided to invite Jim to take on a small consulting project. This gave both of them the opportunity to explore what might develop naturally – an option neither had considered prior to our conversation.

WHY THIS WORKED

Had I skipped over Jim's response (his use of 'we') or defaulted to standard career questions, we could easily have missed the *real* conversation we needed to have. By embodying the eight relational principles, however, we created space for honesty, understanding, and awareness. We were able to self- and co-regulate, supporting our emotional and relational wellbeing and preventing the conversation becoming oppositional or indirect.

Presence allowed me to hear Jim in the here and now. **Reflection** allowed us to pause and make meaning from a simple observation, and allowed Jim to both access and process his experience. **Curiosity** led us to the root of

Jim's experience and response. **Vulnerability** enabled us to explore honestly without having to know the outcome. **Respectful candour** allowed me to ask the question and hear what was being *felt*, not just what was being *said*. **Navigating difference** helped us embrace uncertainty and unexpected insights, and we were both **in service of the same goal**: making sure the company hired Jim only if it was the right fit for both of them. In all of this, a **mindset of abundance** opened a path beyond binary options (to hire Jim or not) to co-create the right next step.

Relational leadership in action doesn't just help organisations hire the right people. It helps people discover *if* they are right, *when* they are right, and *how* to engage in a way that's sustainable, energising, and true to who they are.

In addition to the relational principles in this conversation, several **conversational processes** helped us relate to each other effectively in the space between. First, **self-regulation**: by managing my autonomic response (to fill silences, steer the conversation, or jump to conclusions), I was able to stay fully present and attuned to Jim's felt experience. This created a calm, open space where we could both move forward without succumbing to our attachment styles or survival state.

Throughout, I consistently **asked permission** before moving into more reflective questions ('Is this something we can explore a little more?'). This showed Jim I respected his autonomy and that the space between us was psychologically safe.

Clarifying was key in exploring Jim's shifting relationship with burnout; when I invited him to articulate the percentages of burnout versus curiosity, it gave him the language for something he might previously have found hard to express. I also used **mirroring** to reflect his words back to him – especially his repeated use of 'we'. This helped him hear himself in a new way. Finally, I offered **validation** throughout: acknowledging his surprise, his shifting feelings, and his insights as valuable and real. These processes didn't direct or control the conversation. Rather, they *held* it, creating a space in which we could both safely explore, discover, and find clarity about Jim's readiness to take on a new role.

What would have happened if this conversation had occurred without the relational principles above? I might have made up my own story about Jim's use of 'we': *Who does he think he is, talking like he's already got the job? This guy is arrogant.*

Alternatively, I might have taken Jim's language to mean he was entirely on board, advising the CEO to hire him for the role without further question. In time, that relationship might have unravelled as Jim returned to his old patterns of overwork and burnout. This could have resulted in a rehire within a short period of time.

Your interactions affect your outcomes. The quality of how we relate to others has an impact on our personal wellbeing and on the wellbeing of the organisation we are in service of. This is what I mean when I say learning to show up in the relational space effectively and with curiosity changes everything.

REWRITING THE SCRIPT FOR A SENIOR EXECUTIVE

I was supporting a Head of People – let's call her Kim – who was struggling with ongoing conflict within one of the organisation's teams. This was centring around a team member we'll call Hannah. Kim described a recurring cycle: Hannah would regularly approach her to 'offload' and 'dump' her frustrations – about colleagues, workloads, or feeling unsupported. Each time, the conversation would follow the same pattern: Hannah would become agitated, share a long stream of issues, leave the meeting with no clear resolution, and return days later in the same emotional state. Kim felt drained, frustrated, and stuck, unable to move the dynamic forward despite genuinely wanting to help.

I wanted to show Kim and Hannah that change doesn't happen in isolation – in this case by 'fixing' Hannah's tendency to dump – but rather in the space between. Hannah had a deep-seated script: *Nothing will change, No one cares enough to do something different, I won't have a different experience.* It was rooted in her anxious attachment style and was being reinforced by a survival state created by the quality of her relationships – including oppositional language, a lack of presence, and a lack of reflection. This was not only affecting Hannah's ability to contribute effectively, it was creating ripple effects across the team.

I encouraged Kim to engage with Hannah differently, using a relational approach grounded in presence, reflection, curiosity, and respectful candour. The key was not to fix the problem, but to interrupt the pattern by changing the quality of the conversation. This meant bringing awareness to the here-and-now experience and supporting Hannah to reflect on what was happening for her, rather than focusing solely on external issues.

The next time Hannah came to offload, Kim self-regulated her frustration and stayed grounded, holding space for something different to emerge. She began with a simple question that caused Hannah to pause to see what she was in service of: 'What would you like to talk about today?'

While Hannah shared, Kim mirrored her words back to ensure clarity, then asked for confirmation, helping her feel heard while also bringing focus to the conversation. Then came the shift: 'What do you need from me in this conversation?'

Hannah paused again, surprised, and said, 'I just need you to listen.'

Kim followed up with: 'How will you know I've listened, and what will it feel like for you?' This brought Hannah into contact with her felt experience – something she hadn't been asked to reflect on before.

As the conversation deepened, Kim asked, 'When you leave here, what do you hope to feel differently as a result of this conversation? Because if you want to have this same conversation in three days, it means today hasn't been valuable. So how can we make it valuable for you?'

Hannah looked visibly taken aback but thoughtful. 'I guess I want to feel less helpless,' she said.

That opened the door for curiosity and reflection: 'And how will that impact the way you show up at work this week? Say I had a video camera following you. What would I see that's different?'

Hannah began to display small, tangible shifts: she was calmer and talked less, she spent more time working than chatting to colleagues, she showed up on time rather than finding excuses to leave the office – the signs of agency and self-regulation emerging.

Finally, Kim checked in to summarise the conversation: 'Do you feel I've really heard you? Is there anything else you need from me right now? What's changed for you as a result of us having this conversation?'

Hannah said, 'I feel calmer. It's weird, but I think just having you ask me those questions made me realise I've been stuck in the same story. Maybe I can try something different.'

WHY THIS WORKED

This interaction embodied the eight relational principles in a powerful way. Kim's presence and self-regulation allowed her to listen, not just to Hannah's words, but to what was happening for her when she dumped her feelings in the relational space. Through reflection and curiosity, she disrupted the familiar script, prompting Hannah to explore her experience instead of looping through blame or frustration. With respectful candour, Kim was willing to name this unhelpful pattern and invite Hannah into accountability – without judgement but with an openness to explore her responsibility in bringing her emotions to work. Both Kim and Hannah engaged with vulnerability – for Kim, by stepping away from problem-solving and into a relational process, and for Hannah, by confronting the impact of her behaviours.

Crucially, in all this Kim held a mindset of abundance. Rather than seeing Hannah as a problem, she viewed the conversation as an opportunity for growth and connection. By focusing on being in service of a shared goal – Hannah's wellbeing and the collaboration of the team – she was able to facilitate Hannah experiencing a different response to conflict and stress.

For the organisation, this shift in the team's ability to relate to each other helped break a cycle of conflict, dependency, and frustration. Hannah began to take more ownership of her emotions and needs, and the team's dynamic improved as her reactivity decreased. Kim reported fewer repetitive 'dumping' conversations and more proactive engagement from Hannah. Importantly, the underlying anxious attachment pattern – the constant seeking of reassurance without resolution – began to shift. All this because Hannah was having a different corrective felt experience: one of being not only listened to, but truly heard.

This example shows how, when we pay attention to language, what we are in service of, our presence and reflection, we can transform not only individual patterns, but the collective health of a team. It also shows we cannot solve conflict by staying on the surface, having the same wrong conversations in reactive loops. Change happens in the space between, and when we step into that space with empathy, we can transform even the most ingrained of stories.

CONCLUSION

ISLANDS OF COHERENCE

I'll let you in on a secret. The principles and processes in this book might have been difficult at times for you to read, but they were also difficult for me to write. This is because I have been painfully aware that I have taken ideas and practices normally used in a therapy room and asked you to apply and embody them at work. It's a big request. As a leader or CEO, the language of this book might feel unfamiliar – even weak. As a colleague, manager, employee, or team member, it might feel embarrassing. In fact, for anyone in a corporate setting, the methods of communicating in this book might not sit easily, particularly if you have a culture already defined by discord and defensiveness.

This is why the principles go beyond words and into the heart. It's why throughout I have not asked you simply to apply them but to *embody* them, allowing yourself not only to practise being in relationship in a regulated and connected way, but to experience what it's like. I hope that as you go forward, when you *feel* the results of reflection, or curiosity, or vulnerability, or respectful candour, and you have the experience of what it's like to ask the right questions instead of assuming you already know, it will matter less what you talk about, and more that you pay attention to what is happening for each of you in that space.

To do this, I have asked you to take a risk. This is because, to be in relationship – to build our capacity to relate to the people around us – we have to take the chance of losing something we currently hold dear. That might be our biases, our stories, our assumptions, or our ideas. It might be the ease with which we settle into our old, familiar survival state, or the attachment style we've come to think of as part of our personalities. It might be our beliefs about other people, or even our beliefs about ourselves. It might be simply our levels of comfort as we start to have conversations that don't feel natural.

But let me ask you this: do you want to create an organisation where people have a sense of belonging? Where people feel safe enough to have the one conversation they need to have instead of skirting around issues that only create more problems? Do you want to build empathy? Do you want to create a culture of effective communication, reciprocity, and self-awareness? If you do – and if you truly, deeply mean it when you say this is your goal – what I'm asking you is not a request, but a necessity.

The reason your culture transformation programmes, your awaydays, your values, and your team bonding haven't worked so far is because most of the time we don't actually take that risk. Change – deep, lasting change – happens only when we have the positive, corrective felt experience of something new inside us and between us.

At the beginning of this book, I explained that we have an epidemic of relational poverty in our workplaces. It's causing a destructive output – of anxiety, stress, low productivity, and disengagement. And yet, rather than addressing the problem at the source, we are still spending our time mitigating the symptoms – applying mental health 'first aid' when the problem is deeper, more insidious, more longstanding, and more entrenched than a quick fix could ever solve.

The answer is not in treating poor mental health at all, but in transforming what causes that poor mental health in the first place: our failure to show up in the space between us and relate to others in the way we're designed to. Instead of focusing on fixing the individual, we need to accept that the problem isn't an individual one to fix.

I appreciate what I'm asking for here is transformative – the principles in this book require you to rethink not only how you communicate and how you relate to those around you, but also how you think about big issues like mental wellbeing, collaboration, and productivity.

Our resistance to change is often precisely because it feels so big. How do we transform the way we relate to each other at scale? Surely a change between two people can't make a difference across an entire organisation? Isn't culture shaped by leadership? Unless leadership is on board, surely nothing will change?

Professor Margaret Mead said, 'Never doubt that a small group of thoughtful, committed citizens can change the world. Indeed, it's the only thing that ever has.' Ultimately, you must choose whether or not you are going to do this work. Does it matter to you enough? But know this: all it takes is for one person to show up differently in an organisation and *everything* changes.

A few days ago I watched as a flock of starlings – I think the proper name is a 'murmuration' – ebbed and flowed across the evening sky. It was the most beautiful sight, thousands of birds moving as one, shifting in perfect harmony together. I thought, *If only organisations could be like that.*

When I watched those thousands of birds creating complex patterns, it made me think of how nature not only successfully coexists in harmony with itself, but does that at scale.

In a murmuration, there isn't a single leader, but rather each bird connects with just six or seven others around it, constantly adjusting in real time. In this way, each of those birds is influenced by the few around it, together becoming the ultimate small team as part of a massive whole. This is how nature manages to cooperate and collaborate in self-organised chaos, even at such a colossal scale.

I believe this is how organisations can scale, too. Change can happen, not through top-down directive, but through distributed belief and connection. When we interact relationally with the people around us, we influence not just those people but the organisation at large, because what happens in the space between two people can trickle out to a wider audience.

In quantum physics there is the term 'islands of coherence'. It refers to the small, localised regions within a larger chaotic or disordered system where order and stability emerge. Despite surrounding randomness or disorder, these pockets create stability and structure. It explains why certain ideas, social movements, or systems thrive, even in disruptive conditions. It's also what enables large, unmanageable groups to shift from one way of being to another.

In organisations, you cannot and will not scale results until you can scale the principles in this book. That starts with the first one. When you change how you show up, everything around you changes. By starting to apply and embody these principles – choosing to have the talk you're avoiding, to encourage connection rather than competition, to find out rather than assume – you can affect every relationship, every conversation, every meeting, and every interaction you have. You become the one person who starts the process of that scale.

Cultural transformation in organisations doesn't start from the top. It starts in small, self-organising pockets. It's less about big initiatives and more about daily behaviours and values – the conversations between teams and individuals who decide to do things differently to how they've always been done.

Imagine a team in a rigid corporate environment deciding to start its meetings with this question: 'What do we hope to get out of today?'

Or imagine a manager choosing to conduct his one-to-ones differently from now on – instead of assessing KPIs, asking 'What was it like for you when that happened?'

Or imagine a board member, at the end of a tough discussion, going around the room and asking 'What's landed for you here, and who else needs to know about this in order to get things done?'

What if it's not the executives who hold the key to transformation in our organisations, but the smallest of teams? What if it's just you? When we talk about a 'relational process', we so often imagine it as the responsibility of us both. Yet what if just one person can influence a change? The reality is that, in any given conversation or interaction, one person may arrive fully open while the other remains guarded, distracted, or dysregulated. But what if one of you shows up first? What if one of you is willing to hold the space, to offer steadiness?

You can become the regulating force in the space between, the grounded presence that invites the other into coherence. When you offer steadiness, you create an environment where the other person can move from fragmentation to connection – not by force, but by the quiet pull of stability. In other words, you're not *responsible* for their regulation, but you can be the invitation. The freedom that comes with this is transformational for you both because to be in service in this way is not to lose yourself, but to expand the possibility of what is shared and created.

We're used to thinking of interactions as the coming together of two separate entities. In one way this is true: at first we meet as separate, subjective beings, each carrying our own stories, attachment styles, survival state, and unconscious patterns. Whether anxious, avoidant, or disorganised, we show up as we are, shaped by our past experiences of either connection or disconnection. Yet when we show up effectively in the space between, something shifts. A different kind of conversation becomes possible – a different way of meeting altogether.

This is where we enter the 'transpersonal' – a space beyond words, beyond exchange, beyond transaction, beyond right and wrong. It is Rumi's 'field', a place where something larger than both of us emerges, where heart and mind, logic and emotion, individual and collective begin to weave together. In that weaving, we don't just communicate. We transform.

I don't use the word 'transpersonal' lightly. It's not an abstract idea, but a felt experience – the stepping into a reality different from our own. It's a space where the nervous system exhales, where we move beyond survival into trust, where what was ruptured becomes repaired. It's here we find love – not in the sentimental sense, but in the deepest, most essential way: love as safety, love as creation, love as a new form of collaboration. And all this begins with one person being willing to hold the space.

Perhaps, today, that person is you.

Love is the unconditional determination to understand a person so they can understand themselves.[21]

While organisations may appear an unconventional setting for love, I firmly believe that fostering an environment steeped in understanding, compassion, reflection, presence, curiosity, service, and care is the key to unlocking success on all fronts – relational and economic alike. This book is, in essence, the science of love, and my deepest hope is that you've encountered it within these pages.

NOTES

1. https://about.google/community-guidelines/, accessed 16 June 2025
2. J. Moore, LinkedIn post (2023), https://www.linkedin.com/posts/justin-moore-468145b8_so-after-over-165-years-at-google-i-appear-activity-7022217049342902273-aVlF/, accessed 16 June 2025
3. Deloitte, *Mental Health and Employers* (3 May 2024), https://deloitte.com/uk/en/services/consulting/research/mental-health-and-employers-the-case-for-employers-to-invest-in-supporting-working-parents-and-a-mentally-health-workplace.html, accessed 16 June 2025
4. D. J. Siegel, *The Developing Mind: How Relationships and the Brain Interact to Shape Who We Are, Second Edition* (Guilford Press, 2012)
5. J. Paxman, 'David Bowie Speaks to Jeremy Paxman on BBC Newsnight' (*Newsnight*, 1999), https://www.youtube.com/watch?v=FiK7s_0tGsg, accessed 16 June 2025
6. D. J. Siegel, *Brainstorm: The Power and Purpose of the Teenage Brain* (Scribe UK, 2014), p. 53
7. D. Spiegel et al, 'Brief Structured Respiration Practices Enhance Mood and Reduce Physiological Arousal', *Cell Reports Medicine*, 4/1 (2023), https://pubmed.ncbi.nlm.nih.gov/36630953/, accessed 16 June 2025
8. M. Manassi and D. Whitney, 'Our brains Keep Us 15 Seconds "In The Past" to Help Us See a Stable World, Says Study' *ScienceAlert* (30 January 2022), https://www.sciencealert.com/to-help-us-see-a-stable-world-our-brains-keep-us-15-seconds-in-the-past, accessed 6 June 2025
9. Insights, *Leadership in a Psychologically Safe Workplace* (no date), https://www.insights.com/media/3300/insights-how-to-lead-a-psychologically-safe-workplace-ebook.pdf, accessed 16 June 2025
10. B. Brown, *Daring Greatly: How the Courage to Be Vulnerable Transforms the Way We Live, Love, Parent, and Lead* (Penguin Life, 2015)
11. S. Khatri, 'Keeping Up with Gen Z: Moving Beyond Stereotypes' (HR Daily Advisor, updated 23 August 2024), https://hrdailyadvisor.com/2024/08/23/keeping-up-with-gen-z-moving-beyond-stereotypes/, accessed 16 June 2025
12. Ciphr, 'Workplace Discrimination Statistics in 2025 | Discrimination at work' (2025), https://www.ciphr.com/infographics/workplace-discrimination-statistics?utm_source=chatgpt.com, accessed 16 June 2025

13. K. Cai, 'Google Scraps Diversity-based Hiring Targets' (Reuters, 26 February 2025), https://www.reuters.com/technology/google-scraps-diversity-based-hiring-targets-wsj-reports-2025-02-05/?utm_source=chatgpt.com, accessed 16 June 2025

14. Financial Times, June 2024. "Rescuing diversity from the DEI backlash." https://www.ft.com/content/18a8e9c4-d515-4d9b-aac1-d88c02b46028?utm, accessed 16 June 2025

15. Sainsbury Wellcome Centre, 'Neuroscientists Decode the Brain's Response to Unexpected Sensory Inputs' (News Medical, 28 August 2025), https://www.news-medical.net/news/20240828/Neuroscientists-decode-the-braine28099s-response-to-unexpected-sensory-inputs.aspx, accessed 16 June 2025

16. J. Haidt, 'Monomania Is Illiberal and Stupefying' (Persuasion, 1 October 2021), https://www.persuasion.community/p/haidt-monomania-is-illiberal-and, accessed 16 June 2025.

17. A. Wrzesniewski, J. E. Dutton, G. Debebe, *Interpersonal Sensemaking and the Meaning of Work, Research in Organizational Behavior*, 25 (2003), 93–135, https://www.sciencedirect.com/science/article/abs/pii/S0191308503250036, accessed 16 June 2025

18. https://www.qualtrics.com/m/www.xminstitute.com/wp-content/uploads/2017/03/XMI_EmployeeEngagementBenchmarkStudy-2017.pdf?ty=mktocd-thank-you, accessed 16 June 2025

19. The Open University, 'Personal Branding for Career Success, Week 2, Values, Vision and personality' (no date), https://www.open.edu/openlearn/mod/oucontent/view.php?id=78689§ion=3, accessed 16 June 2025

20. G. Diniz et al, 'The Effects of Gratitude Interventions: A Systematic Review and Meta-analysis' (Einstein, Sao Paulo, 21, 2023), https://pmc.ncbi.nlm.nih.gov/articles/PMC10393216/, accessed 16 June 2025

21. Vietnamese monk Thich Nhat Hanh.